SCENES FOR TWO

This extraordinary collection was designed to fill an essential need: short, playable, diverse scenes for acting students.

Each scene was chosen for its intrinsic excellence as it stands alone from the rest of the play. In addition, every selection represents part of the tremendous range of styles from great Greek drama to modern American realism and surrealism.

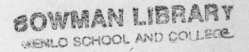

Bantam Books of Related Interest
Ask your bookseller for the books you have missed

AUDITION by Michael Shurtleff
BRIAN'S SONG by William Blinn
50 GREAT SCENES FOR STUDENT ACTORS edited by
    Lewy Olfson
FILM SCENES FOR ACTORS by Joshua Karton
FOR COLORED GIRLS WHO HAVE CONSIDERED SUICIDE
    WHEN THE RAINBOW IS ENUF by Ntozake Shange
INHERIT THE WIND by Jerome Lawrence and
    Robert E. Lee
THE MIRACLE WORKER by William Gibson
MODERN AMERICAN SCENES FOR STUDENT ACTORS
    edited by Wynn Handman
THE MOUSETRAP AND OTHER PLAYS by Agatha Christie
THE NIGHT THOREAU SPENT IN JAIL by
    Jerome Lawrence and Robert E. Lee
SAM SHEPHERD: SEVEN PLAYS by Sam Shepard

50
GREAT SCENES
FOR
STUDENT ACTORS

Edited by Lewy Olfson

BANTAM BOOKS
TORONTO • NEW YORK • LONDON • SYDNEY • AUCKLAND

For the De Flumeres:
Ed, Barbara, Tom, and Amy

RL 5, IL age 9 and up

50 GREAT SCENES FOR STUDENT ACTORS

Bantam edition / January 1970
12 printings through April 1980

ACKNOWLEDGMENTS

Contents

Acknowledgments   *v*
Introduction   *xi*

Part One:
SCENES FOR ONE MAN AND ONE WOMAN

From *The Time of Your Life* by William Saroyan
     3
From *I Am a Camera* by John Van Druten   12
From *The Way of the World* by William Congreve
     18
From *The Sleeping Prince* by Terence Rattigan
     24
From *A Moon for the Misbegotten* by Eugene O'Neill
     29
From *Fashion* by Anna Cora Mowatt   34
From *Orpheus Descending* by Tennessee Williams
     39
From *The Second Man* by S. N. Behrman   45
From *A Doll's House* by Henrik Ibsen   51
From *Cymbeline* by William Shakespeare   58
From *The Circle* by W. Somerset Maugham   67
From *Uncle Vanya* by Anton Chekov   75
From *The Autumn Garden* by Lillian Hellman
     79
From *Patience* by W. S. Gilbert   85

From *Secret Service* by William Gillette   90

From *Arms and the Man* by George Bernard Shaw
        97

From *Medea* by Euripides   101

From *The Road to Rome* by Robert Sherwood
        106

From *Lady Windermere's Fan* by Oscar Wilde
        111

From *Venus Observed* by Christopher Fry   117

From *The Magnificent Yankee* by Emmet Lavery
        122

From *The Cage* by Mario Fratti   127

From *Scuba Duba* by Bruce Jay Friedman   132

From *Goat Song* by Franz Werfel   138

Part Two:
SCENES FOR TWO MEN

From *Edward, My Son,* by Robert Morley and Noel
        Langley   145

From *The Master Builder* by Henrik Ibsen   153

From *A Woman of No Importance* by Oscar Wilde
        160

From *The Seventh Seal* by Ingmar Bergman   168

From *The Waltz of the Toreadors* by Jean Anouilh
        172

From *The Two Gentlemen of Verona* by William
        Shakespeare   176

From *Daisy Miller* by Henry James   182

From *The Barber of Seville* by Beaumarchais
        191

From *The Duenna* by Richard Brinsley Sheridan
        197

From *Lamp at Midnight* by Barrie Stavis   204

From *The Relapse* by Sir John Vanbrugh   *209*
From *The Deputy* by Rolf Hochhuth   *216*
From *Death of a Salesman* by Arthur Miller   *221*

Part Three:
SCENES FOR TWO WOMEN

From *The Autumn Garden* by Lillian Hellman
    231
From *Pride and Prejudice* by Helen Jerome   *237*
From *The Women* by Clare Boothe   *243*
From *Uncle Vanya* by Anton Chekov   *248*
From *The Vortex* by Nöel Coward   *253*
From *Trifles* by Susan Glaspell   *262*
From *Socrates Wounded* by Alfred Levinson
    266
From *The Chalk Garden* by Enid Bagnold   *271*
From *The Ladies of the Corridor* by Dorothy Parker
    and Arnaud d'Usseau   *279*
From *Separate Tables* by Terence Rattigan   *285*
From *Autumn Crocus* by C. L. Anthony   *291*
From *Romeo and Juliet* by William Shakespeare
    300
From *Mary of Scotland* by Maxwell Anderson
    306

Index of Titles and Authors   *317*

Introduction

The student actor's need for good scenes is seemingly endless. In most first-year courses in acting given at the college level, a scene is due for presentation in class every other week. The high-school student electing a course in acting and the student enrolled in an independent acting school or workshop are under only slightly less pressure to prepare a succession of scenes. No sooner has one scene been presented, another must be found. It was to help meet this need for a handy selection of scenes to choose from that this book was prepared.

It should be noted at once that the selection of scenes presented here reflects primarily the editor's own tastes. There are probably as many sets of criteria for evaluating any scene's usefulness as there are teachers of acting. No claims are made, therefore, that the student actor will find every scene here of equal value to him. These scenes are, essentially, the kind that I found useful when I taught acting at the Boston Center for Adult Education, and that earlier I had found useful when I was a drama student at Carnegie Institute of Technology (now Carnegie-

Mellon University). They and their kind have worked for me; it is my belief that they will work for many others.

Every scene in this anthology did have to meet certain objective criteria. Only two-person scenes were acceptable; the practical difficulty of a student's being able to meet with two other students for a sufficient number of rehearsals to prepare the scene adequately precluded use of any three-person scenes. As far as possible, the two roles in a scene had to be fairly and equally divided, so that both actors using the scene could take full advantage of the scene as a learning experience. And the grouping of scenes had to represent a balance of dramatic styles, types, and acting problems. Some scenes lend themselves best to work on truthful talking and listening, some to characterization, some to playing an objective, and so forth.

Out of respect to the playwrights, no scene in this collection has been in any way abridged or edited; even individual idiosyncrasies of spelling and punctuation have been maintained. (Minor cuts in stage business have occasionally been made when their inclusion seemed confusing rather than clarifying.) And though in every case a scene can only be fully understood by a reading of the complete play from which it comes, I have tried to choose only scenes that have a degree of self-contained shape, so that rehearsed and presented out of context they will still make dramatic sense.

A few words are in order about scenes *not* included. Although there is no such thing as a scene that "everybody" knows, I have tried to choose scenes that I suspect are unfamiliar to many students, and that are therefore not done to death. Is there anywhere a student actor who needs to be directed to the soda fountain scene from *Our Town*? The recognition scene from *Anastasia*? The Laura-Amanda or Laura-Gentleman Caller scenes from *The Glass Menagerie*? I doubt it.

For the same reason, I have seldom used more than one scene from a given play (there are a few exceptions); because the student is urged to read in its entirety any play from which he intends to present a scene, it is assumed that he will find for himself other good scenes to use. To encourage the student to do this reading, I have often indicated in the notes to a scene that there are other scenes from the same play—or other plays by the same playwright—that will be helpful. (For this reason, women should read at least the introductory notes to the scenes for men, and men the notes to the scenes for women.)

The realities of copyright law also precluded the use of certain scenes. I can only hope that students will find these scenes that I would like to have included through their own reading of world dramatic literature.

The book is divided into three parts: Scenes for One Man and One Woman, Scenes for Two Men, and Scenes for Two Women. Within each of these parts, the scenes are presented in random order—that is, neither chronologically nor in degree of difficulty. It is my hope that students will therefore be compelled to read a number of scenes before making their selection; they will thus be introduced to plays and playwrights that they might not otherwise encounter.

No attempt has been made to tell students how to play a given scene (though I haven't been able to resist dropping an occasional hint about how *not* to play a scene). There is, of course, no "right" way to play a role; and how one approaches a scene for class presentation depends largely upon the acting problem one is dealing with. Remember, though, that these scenes all come from real plays; they were not written as classroom acting exercises. A student ignores the larger context in which the scene is set at his own peril. Again, the best advice is: read the entire play! (All of the plays represented in this collection are currently available in complete published editions, many of them in paperback.)

To one completing work on a manuscript, the sense of obligation and gratitude toward others for their help is enormous. Such debts can only be acknowledged; they cannot be paid. My gratitude, then, to: Dorothy McKittrick, Mary Mapes, and Ellen Krieger, who initiated me into the dark mysteries of Rights and Permissions; Betsy Nordstrom, formerly of Bantam Books, and Gregory Armstrong, still of Bantam Books, for their patience, forbearance, and encouragement; William Saroyan and Alfred Levinson, playwrights represented in this collection, whose correspondence with me about their scenes were highlights of pleasure; Nancy and Bill Dickinson, for courtesies too numerous to list; Ken Olfson, who as an actor gave of his knowledge and as a brother of his understanding. Thanks, thanks, and ever thanks.

Lewy Olfson

50
Great Scenes
for
Student Actors

part 1

**Scenes for
One Man,
One Woman**

The Time of Your Life

By WILLIAM SAROYAN

The plays of William Saroyan are character-ized by a delicate—almost fragile—tender-ness. The fact that scenes such as this one seem artless simplicity itself should not mis-lead you into thinking they are simple to perform. They require great acting skill.

The scene is Nick's Pacific Street Saloon, Restaurant, and Entertainment Palace. Joe and Mary are seated at separate tables, he eyeing the initials on her purse. This scene opens Act II.

(An excellent scene for two men comes later in this Act, between Joe and Kit Carson, beginning with the line, "I don't suppose you ever fell in love with a midget weighing thirty-nine pounds?")

JOE: Is it Madge—Laubowitz?

MARY: Is what *what?*

JOE: Is the name Mabel Lepescu?

MARY: What name?

JOE: The name the initials M. L. stand for. The initials on your bag.

MARY: No.

JOE (*After a long pause, thinking deeply what the name might be, turning a card, looking into the beautiful face of the woman*): Margie Longworthy?

MARY (*All this is very natural and sincere, no comedy on the part of the people involved; they are both solemn, being drunk*): No.

JOE (*His voice higher-pitched, as though he were growing alarmed*): Midge Laurie? (MARY *shakes her head.*)

JOE: My initials are J. T.

MARY (*Pause*): John?

JOE: No. (*Pause.*) Martha Lancaster?

MARY: No. (*Pause.*) Joseph?

JOE: Well, not exactly. That's my first name, but everybody calls me Joe. The last name is the tough one. I'll help you a little. I'm Irish. (*Pause.*) Is it just plain Mary?

MARY: Yes, it is. I'm Irish, too. At least on my father's side. English on my mother's side.

JOE: I'm Irish on both sides. Mary's one of my favorite names. I guess that's why I didn't think of it. I met a girl in Mexico City named Mary once. She was an American from Philadelphia. She got married there. In Mexico City, I mean. While I was there. We were in love too. At least *I* was. You never know about anyone else. They were engaged, you see, and her mother was with her, so they went through with it. Must have been six or seven years ago. She's probably got three or four children by this time.

MARY: Are you still in love with her?

JOE: Well—no. To tell you the truth, I'm not sure. I guess I am. I didn't even know she was engaged until a couple of days before they got married. I thought *I* was going to marry her. I kept thinking all the time about the kind of kids we would be likely to have. My favorite was the third one. The first two were fine. Handsome and fine and intelligent, but that third one was different. Dumb and goofy-looking. I liked *him* a lot. When she told me she was going to be married, I didn't feel so bad about the first two, it was that dumb one.

MARY (*After a pause of some few seconds*): What do you do?

JOE: Do? To tell you the truth, nothing.

MARY: Do you always drink a great deal?

JOE (*Scientifically*): Not always. Only when I'm awake. I sleep seven or eight hours every night, you know.

MARY: How nice. I mean to drink when you're awake.

JOE (*Thoughtfully*): It's a privilege.

MARY: Do you really *like* to drink?

JOE (*Positively*): As much as I like to *breathe*.

MARY (*Beautifully*): Why?

JOE (*Dramatically*): Why do I like to drink? (*Pause.*) Because I don't like to be gypped. Because I don't like to be dead most of the time and just a little alive every once in a long while. (*Pause.*) If I don't drink, I become fascinated by unimportant things— like everybody else. I get busy. Do things. All kinds of little stupid things, for all kinds of little stupid reasons. Proud, selfish, *ordinary* things. I've done them. Now I don't do anything. *I live all the time.* Then I go to sleep.

MARY (*Pause*): Do you sleep well?

JOE (*Taking it for granted*): Of course.

MARY (*Quietly, almost with tenderness*): What are your plans?

JOE (*Loudly, but also tenderly*): Plans? I haven't got any. *I just get up.*

MARY (*Beginning to understand everything*): Oh, yes. Yes, of course.

JOE (*Thoughtfully*): Why do I drink?
(*Pause, while he thinks about it. The thinking appears to be profound and complex, and has the effect of giving his face a very comical and naive expression.*)

JOE: That question calls for a pretty complicated answer. (*He smiles abstractedly.*)

MARY: Oh, I didn't mean—

JOE (*Swiftly, gallantly*): No. No. I *insist*. I *know* why. It's just a matter of finding words. Little ones.

MARY: It really doesn't matter.

JOE (*Seriously*): Oh, yes it does. (*Clinically*): Now, why do I drink? (*Scientifically*): No. Why does *any-body* drink? (*Working it out.*) Every day has twenty-four hours.

MARY (*Sadly but brightly*): Yes, that's true.

JOE: Twenty-four hours. Out of the twenty-four hours at *least* twenty-three and a half are—my God, I don't know why—dull, dead, boring, empty, and murderous. Minutes on the clock, not time of living. It doesn't make any difference who you are or what you do, twenty-three and a half hours of the twenty-four are spent *waiting*.

MARY: Waiting?

JOE (*Gesturing, loudly*): And the more you wait, the less there is to wait for.

MARY (*Attentively, beautifully his student*): Oh?

JOE (*Continuing*): That goes on for days and days, and weeks and months and years, and years, and the first thing you know *all* the years are dead. You yourself are dead. There's nothing to wait for any more. Nothing except minutes on the clock. No time of life. Nothing but minutes, and idiocy. Beautiful, bright, intelligent idiocy. (*Pause.*) Does that answer your question?

MARY (*Earnestly*): I'm afraid it does. Thank you. You shouldn't have gone to all the trouble.

JOE: No trouble at all. (*Pause.*) You have children?

MARY: Yes. Two. A son and a daughter.

JOE (*Delighted*): How swell. Do they look like you?

MARY: Yes.

JOE: Then why are you sad?

MARY: I was always sad. It's just that after I was married I was allowed to drink.

JOE (*Eagerly*): Who are you waiting for?

MARY: No one.

JOE (*Smiling*): I'm not waiting for anybody, either.

MARY: My husband, of course.

JOE: Oh, sure.

MARY: He's a lawyer.

JOE (*Standing, leaning on the table*): He's a great guy. I like him. I'm very fond of him.

MARY (*Listening*): You have responsibilities?

JOE (*Loudly*): *One*, and *thousands*. As a matter of fact, I feel responsible to everybody. At least to everybody I meet. I've been trying for three years to find out if it's possible to live what I think is a civilized life. I mean a life that can't hurt any other life.

MARY: You're famous?

JOE: Very. Utterly unknown, but very famous. Would you like to dance?

MARY: All right.

JOE (*Loudly*): I'm sorry. I don't dance. I didn't think you'd like to.

MARY: To tell you the truth, I don't like to dance at all.

JOE (*Proudly—Commentator*): I can hardly walk.

MARY: You mean you're tight?

JOE (*Smiling*): No. I mean *all* the time.

MARY (*Looking at him closely*): Were you ever in Paris?

JOE: In 1929, and again in 1934.

MARY: What month of 1934?

JOE: Most of April, all of May, and a little of June.

MARY: I was there in November and December that year.

JOE: We were there almost at the same time. You were married?

MARY: Engaged.
(*They are silent a moment, looking at one another.*)

MARY (*Quietly and with great charm*): Are you *really* in love with me?

JOE: Yes.

MARY: Is it the champagne?

JOE: Yes. Partly, at least. (*He sits down.*)

MARY: If you don't see me again will you be very unhappy?

JOE: Very.

MARY (*Getting up*): I'm so pleased.
(*JOE is deeply grieved that she is going. In fact, he is almost panic-stricken about it, getting up in a way that is full of furious sorrow and regret.*)

MARY: I must go now. Please don't get up.
(JOE *is up, staring at her with amazement.*)

MARY: Good-by.

JOE (*Simply*): Good-by.
(MARY *stands looking at him a moment, then turns and goes.* JOE *stands staring after her for a long time.*)

FROM **I Am a Camera**

By JOHN VAN DRUTEN

In this play, set in the Berlin of the 1930's, Van Druten created a truly unforgettable character in Sally Bowles. No less interesting is the character of Chris, based on Christopher Isherwood, whose Berlin sketches provided the original impetus for the play. Sally and Chris have genuine feelings for each other, but they are doomed by their inadequacies not to find permanent happiness together.

In this, the final scene of the play, Chris is packing his trunk, preparatory to leaving Berlin, when Sally, who had left him, bursts in. (Also of interest is the Chris-Sally scene in Act I, Scene 2, in which Sally announces that she is going to have a baby.)

SALLY (*Entering*): Chris!

CHRIS: Sally! I thought you'd gone. I thought you'd gone home.

SALLY: No. Mother left this morning.

CHRIS: And you're not going?

SALLY: Not home. Oh, Chris, it was ghastly getting rid of Mother. But I knew I had to, after that scene here.

CHRIS: How did you do it?

SALLY (*Giggling*): I did something awful. I got a friend in London to send her an anonymous telegram telling her Daddy was having an affair. That sent her off in a mad whirl. But Daddy will forgive me. Besides, it's probably true—and I don't blame him. I told Mother I'd follow her when I got some business settled. And something will turn up to stop it. It always does, for me. I'm all right, Chris. I'm back again.

CHRIS: (*Smiling*): Yes. I can see you are.

SALLY: Is there anything to drink?

CHRIS: There's just a little gin, that's all.

SALLY: I'd love a little gin. In a tooth glass. Flavored with peppermint. Where are you off to?

CHRIS: I *am* going home.

SALLY: When?

CHRIS: Tomorrow night. I'm going to Fritz and Natalia's wedding in the afternoon.

SALLY: Wedding? How did that happen?

CHRIS: Fritz told Natalia about himself, and that did it. And now he doesn't have to pretend any more. Come with me, Sally. They'd love to see you.

SALLY: Oh, I'd like to, but I won't be here.

CHRIS: Where will you be?

SALLY: I'm leaving for the Riviera tonight.

CHRIS: With whom?

SALLY: For a picture.

CHRIS: Well, fine. Is it a good part?

SALLY: I don't really know. I expect so. You haven't got a drink, Chris. Have a drop of this. Make it a loving cup. (*He takes a sip.*) Why are you going away, Chris?

CHRIS: Because I'll never write as long as I'm here. And I've got to write. It's the only thing I give a damn about. I don't regret the time I've spent here. I wouldn't have missed a single hangover of it. But now I've got to put it all down—what I think about it. And live by it, too, if I can. Thank you for the idea about that book, Sally. The short stories. I think maybe that will work out.

SALLY: Oh, I hope so. I do want you to be good, Chris.

CHRIS: I am going to try, Sally. Now, tell me about you and this job that you don't seem to know anything about. Or care about. Who's the man, Sally?

SALLY: Man?

CHRIS: Oh, come off it.

SALLY (*Giggling a little*): Well, there is a man. He's wonderful, Chris. He really is.

CHRIS: Where did you meet him?

SALLY: Two days ago. Just after we left here. He saw us in the street ... Mother and me, I mean—and our eyes met—his and mine, I mean—and he sort of followed us. To a tea shop, where he sat and gazed at me. And back to the hotel. And at the restaurant. He had the table next to us, and he kept sort of hitching his foot around my chair. And he passed me a note in the fruit-basket. Only Mother got it by mistake. But it was in German. I told her it was from a movie agent. And I went over and talked to him, and he *was!* Then we met later. He's quite marvellous, Chris. He's got a long, black beard. Well, not really long. I've never been kissed by a beard before. I thought it would be awful. But it isn't. It's quite exciting. Only he doesn't speak much German. He's a Yugoslavian. That's why I don't know much about the picture. But I'm sure it will be all right. He'll write in something. And now I've got to run.

CHRIS: Oh, Sally, *must* you? Must you go on like this? Why don't you go home, too? Come back with me. I mean it, Sally. My family'll give me some money if I'm home. Or I'll get a job. I'll see that you're all right.

SALLY: It wouldn't be any good, Chris. I'd run away from you, too. The moment anything attractive came along. It's all right for you. You're a writer. You really are. I'm not even an actress, really. I'd love to see my name in lights, but even if I had a first-night tomorrow, if something exciting turned up, I'd go after it. I can't help it. That's me. I'm sentimental enough to hope that one day I'll meet the perfect man, and marry him and have an enormous family and be happy, but until then—well, that's how I am. You know that really, don't you?

CHRIS: Yes, Sally, I'm afraid I do.

SALLY: Afraid? Oh, Chris, am I too awful—for *me*, I mean?

CHRIS: No, Sally. I'm very fond of you.

SALLY: I do hope you are. Because I am of you. Was it true about eternal friendship that we swore?

CHRIS: Yes, of course it was. Really true. Tell me, do you have an address?

SALLY: No, I don't. But I'll write. I really will. Postcards and everything. And you write to me. Of course, you'll be writing all sorts of things—books and things—that I can read. Will you dedicate one to me?

CHRIS: The very first one.

SALLY: Oh, good. Perhaps that'll be my only claim to fame. Well—good-bye for now, Chris. Neck and leg-break.

CHRIS: Neck and leg-break. (*They go into each other's arms.*)

SALLY: (*Starts to go, then turns to* CHRIS): I do love you. (*She goes out swiftly.*)

CHRIS (*Stares after her, for a moment*): I love you too, Sally. And it's so damned stupid that that's not enough to keep two people together.

FROM **The Way of the World**

By WILLIAM CONGREVE

The Restoration Drama, perhaps more than any other body of dramatic literature, demands a flawlessness of acting technique if it is to be successful. The style is everything—and if it is not brilliant, brittle, polished, and graceful, it is nothing.

This scene, in which Mirabell and Mrs. Millamant exchange conditions for marriage, could serve as the prototype for the highest Restoration style.

MIRABELL: Do you lock yourself up from me, to make my search more curious? Or is this pretty artifice contrived to signify that here the chase must end, and my pursuit be crowned, for you can fly no further?

MILLAMANT: Vanity! No—I'll fly and be followed to the last moment. Though I am upon the very verge of matrimony, I expect you should solicit me as much as if I were wavering at the gate of a monastery, with one foot over the threshold. I'll be solicited to the very last, nay, and afterwards.

MIRABELL: What, after the last?

MILLAMANT: Oh, I should think I was poor and had nothing to bestow, if I were reduced to an inglorious ease, and freed from the agreeable fatigues of solicitation.

MIRABELL: But do not you know, that when favors are conferred upon instant and tedious solicitation, that they diminish in their value, and that both the giver loses the grace, and the receiver lessens his pleasure?

MILLAMANT: It may be in things of common application, but never sure in love. Oh, I hate a lover that can dare to think he draws a moment's air independent on the bounty of his mistress. There is not so impudent a thing in nature as the saucy look of an assured man, confident of success. The pedantic arrogance of a very husband has not so pragmatical an air. Ah! I will never marry, unless I am first made sure of my will and pleasure.

MIRABELL: Would you have 'em both before marriage? Or will you be contented with the first now, and stay for the other till after grace?

MILLAMANT: Ah, don't be impertinent. —My dear liberty, shall I leave thee? My faithful solitude, my darling contemplation, must I bid you then adieu? Ay-h, adieu—my morning thoughts, agreeable wakings, indolent slumbers, all ye *douceurs*, ye *sommeils du matin*, adieu? —I can't do't, 'tis more than impossible. Positively, Mirabell, I'll lie abed in a morning as long as I please.

MIRABELL: Then I'll get up in a morning as early as I please.

MILLAMANT: Ah! Idle creature, get up when you will. —And d'ee hear, I won't be called names after I'm married; positively I won't be called names.

MIRABELL: Names?

MILLAMANT: Ay, as wife, spouse, my dear, joy, jewel, love, sweetheart, and the rest of that nauseous cant, in which men and their wives are so fulsomely familiar—I shall never bear that. —Good Mirabell, don't let us be familiar or fond, nor kiss before folks, like my Lady Fadler and Sir Francis; nor go to Hyde Park together the first Sunday in a new chariot, to provoke eyes and whispers, and then never to be seen together again, as if we were proud of one another the first week, and ashamed of one another for ever after. Let us never visit together, nor go to a play together, but let us be very strange and well bred. Let us be as strange as if we had been married a great while, and as well bred as if we were not married at all.

MIRABELL: Have you any more conditions to offer? Hitherto your demands are pretty reasonable.

MILLAMANT: Trifles, —as liberty to pay and receive visits to and from whom I please; to write and receive letters, without interrogatories or wry faces on your part. To wear what I please, and choose conversation with regard only to my own taste; to have no obligation upon me to converse with wits that I don't like, because they are your acquaintance; or to be intimate with fools, because they may be your relations. Come to dinner when I please, dine in my dressing-room when I'm out of humor, without giving a reason. To have my closet inviolate; to be sole empress of my tea-table, which you must never presume to approach without first asking leave. And lastly, wherever I am, you shall always knock at the door before you come in. These articles subscribed, if I continue to endure you a little longer, I may by degrees dwindle into a wife.

MIRABELL: Your bill of fare is something advanced in this latter account. Well, have I liberty to offer conditions—that when you are dwindled into a wife I may not be beyond measure enlarged into a husband?

MILLAMANT: You have free leave; propose your utmost; speak and spare not.

MIRABELL: I thank you. *Imprimis*, then, I covenant that your acquaintance be general; that you admit no sworn confidante or intimate of your own sex; no she-friend to screen her affairs under your countenance and tempt you to make trial of a mutual secrecy. No decoy-duck to wheedle you a fop-scrambling to the play in a mask—then bring you home in a pretended fright, when you think you shall be found out—and rail at me for missing the play and disappointing the frolic which you had, to pick me up and prove my constancy.

MILLAMANT: Detestable *imprimis!* I go to the play in a mask!

MIRABELL: *Item*, I article, that you continue to like your own face as long as I shall; and while it passes current with me, that you endeavor not to new-coin it. To which end, together with all vizards for the day, I prohibit all masks for the night, made of oiled-skins and I know not what—hog's bones, hare's gall, pig-water, and the marrow of a roasted cat. In short, I forbid all commerce with the gentlewoman in What-d'ye-call-it Court. *Item*, I shut my doors against all bawds with baskets, and pennyworths of muslin, china, fans, atlases, etc. —*Item*, when you shall be breeding—

MILLAMANT: Ah! name it not.

MIRABELL: Which may be presumed, with a blessing on our endeavors—

MILLAMANT: Odious endeavors!

MIRABELL: I denounce against all strait lacing, squeezing for a shape, till you mold my boy's head like a sugar-loaf, and instead of a man-child, make me the father to a crooked billet. Lastly, to the dominion of the tea-table I submit, —but with proviso, that you exceed not in your province; but restrain yourself to native and simple tea-table drinks, as tea, chocolate, and coffee, as likewise to genuine and authorized tea-table talk—such as mending of fashions, spoiling reputations, railing at absent friends, and so forth—but that on no account you encroach upon the men's prerogative, and presume to drink healths, or toast fellows; for prevention of which I banish all foreign forces, all auxiliaries to the tea-table, as orange-brandy, all aniseed, cinnamon, citron, and Barbadoes waters, together with ratafia and the most noble spirit of clary, —but for cowslip wine, poppy water, and all dormitives, those I allow. These provisos admitted, in other things I may prove a tractable and complying husband.

MILLAMANT: Oh, horrid provisos! filthy strong waters! I toast fellows, other men! I hate your odious provisos.

MIRABELL: Then we're agreed. Shall I kiss your hand upon the contract?

The Sleeping Prince

By TERENCE RATTIGAN

Light without being superficial, sentimental without being maudlin, this story of an unfulfilled love affair between a young chorus girl and a middle-aged member of royalty requires a light touch and deft playing of its actors. (In the film version, the roles were played by Marilyn Monroe and Sir Laurence Olivier.) In spite of their flippancy, the characters must be believably human if they are to be touching.

This scene is from Act II, Scene 3; an earlier scene in the play—the one between the Regent and Peter Northbrook—is an excellent choice for two men.

(THE REGENT *turns to* MARY. *She comes slowly forward.*)

MARY: Good morning.

REGENT: Good morning. (*They embrace fervently.*) My dear, I have been making such a spectacle of my-

self today. Behaving like a schoolboy and—this is so
surprising—loving it. I see now suddenly the truth of
all that you have been saying to me about the joys of
childishness. It is exhilarating.

MARY (*A little sadly*): Yes, it is, isn't it? Oh, dear!
So this morning it's for me to be the grown-up one,
is it?

REGENT: How? Grown-up?

MARY: Darling—listen—you don't need to send
Peter Northbrook out for a special passport. My own
is quite good enough to take me to Carpathia when
I come there. And what's more, my darling, I've found
out the name of a good cheap pension to stay at—
the Villa Malmaison—only just outside the city—

REGENT: But what nonsense is this? Pension? Do
you not realize what I am preparing for you on your
arrival?

MARY (*Sadly*): No. Tell me, please. I'd love to hear.

REGENT: The Sonia Residenz, an enchanting house
in the late Renaissance style—quite little—you will
only need ten or fifteen servants—with a few hundred
acres of park and a most beautiful garden, on a lake,
with the mountains close by. It was built by a six-
teenth-century ancestor of mine—for his favorite
mistress—

MARY: And has been used by his twentieth-century
descendant before now, huh?

REGENT: Well— (*He makes a gesture.*) But never for long.

MARY: I know, my darling. (*She kisses him on the cheek.*) That's just what I mean.

REGENT (*Explosively, pulling her round to face him*): But *Herrgott nochmal!* For not one of the others have I felt any small part of what I now feel for you.

MARY (*Gently*): Yes. And for how long will you feel it, darling?

REGENT: For life.

MARY (*Briskly*): Good. And so will I. You can be quite, quite sure of that. So that when my show comes off and I come out to your country and take a room at the Villa Malmaison and drop you a line to say that I'm there—we can go over together to the Sonia Residenz, and I can tell you what I want done to it—because if I'm to stay in it for the rest of my time on earth, I'll need quite a lot done, won't I?
(*Pause. The* REGENT *is looking angry and perplexed.*)

REGENT: When will this show of yours come off?

MARY: Oh, I'd give it another six months.

REGENT: Six months! *Donnerwetter*, girl! Do you not realize what can happen in the course of six months?

MARY (*With resigned acceptance of the facts*): Yes,

darling, only too well. Go on, now, or you'll miss your train.

REGENT: You cannot possibly come before?

MARY: No. But thank you, my darling, so much—so very, very much for asking me.

REGENT (*Pause*): This is good-bye, then?

MARY: Au revoir.

REGENT: Au revoir, of course.
(*There is a pause. A violin can be heard playing outside.*)

REGENT: That *verdammte* music! Did you order it?

MARY: No.

REGENT: Northbrook!

MARY: Maybe. May I have my parting present, now, please?
(*There is a pause. The* REGENT, *at length, shrugs his shoulders, goes to the desk and picks up a case. He hands it to her in silence. She takes the brooch out of its case and makes a slight scratch with her nail.*)

REGENT: What are you doing?

MARY: Just so I'll know which one it is. (*The* REGENT *pins it on.* MARY *looks sadly at the top of his head.*) Poor darling! Do you feel terribly disconcerted?

REGENT: Yes, I do.

MARY (*She kisses him*): Now, go quickly, or I'll cry and that wouldn't be right.
(*The* REGENT *goes to the door and turns to look at her for a long time.*)

REGENT: *Um Gottes willen!* I am nearly crying myself, and that is something I have not done since I was a child.

MARY: Childishness isn't all fun, is it?

REGENT: No. (*He stares at her again.*)

MARY: Anyway, my darling, whatever happens, always remember this. Coming out of a heavenly dream can be a little sad, I grant, but that doesn't make the dream any the less heavenly, does it? Which is another way of saying, thank you, Your Royal Highness, from my heart. (*She curtsies.*)

REGENT (*After a pause*): From my heart, too, Miss Dagenham. I believe I have as much right to that word as yourself. Perhaps more. Who knows?

(*He turns quickly and goes out.*)

FROM **A Moon for the Misbegotten**

By EUGENE O'NEILL

Most of O'Neill's characters—and those in this play are no exception—are great, roaring creatures, filled with violent emotions, robust humor, intense psychological conflicts. Actors are therefore challenged to make his characters larger than life, without resorting to empty flamboyance or exaggerated posturings. (America's greatest playwright was not her most subtle playwright.)

This scene is from the first act of one of O'Neill's less well known plays. Josie, a physical giantess of a woman, is seated on the steps of the Hogan shack, a sawed-off broom handle propped against the wall near her right hand. After a moment, her short, tough father, Hogan, charges around the corner of the house. (Note: The Josie-Hogan scene that opens Act II is equally effective, as is the Josie-Tyrone scene at the end of Act II.)

HOGAN (*Stops as he turns the corner and sees* JOSIE—*furiously*): Where is he? Is he hiding in the house? I'll wipe the floors with him, the lazy bastard! (*Turning his anger against her*): Haven't you a tongue in your head, you great slut you?

JOSIE (*With provoking calm*): Don't be calling me names, you bad-tempered old hornet, or maybe I'll lose my temper, too.

HOGAN: To hell with your temper, you overgrown cow!

JOSIE: I'd rather be a cow than an ugly little buck goat. You'd better sit down and cool off. Old men shouldn't run around raging in the noon sun. You'll get sunstroke.

HOGAN: To hell with sunstroke! Have you seen him?

JOSIE: Have I seen who?

HOGAN: Mike! Who else would I be after, the Pope? He was in the meadow, but the minute I turned my back he sneaked off. (*He sees the pitchfork*.) There's his pitchfork! Will you stop your lying!

JOSIE: I haven't said I didn't see him.

HOGAN: Then don't try to help him hide from me, or— Where is he?

JOSIE: Where you'll never find him.

HOGAN: We'll soon see! I'll bet he's in your room

under the bed, the cowardly lump! (*He moves toward the steps.*)

JOSIE: He's not. He's gone like Thomas and John before him to escape your slave-driving.

HOGAN (*Stares at her incredulously*): You mean he's run off to make his own way in the world?

JOSIE: He has. So make up your mind to it, and sit down.

HOGAN (*Baffled, sits on the boulder and takes off his hat to scratch his head—with a faint trace of grudging respect*): I'd never dream he had that much spunk. (*His temper rising again*): And I know damned well he hadn't, not without you to give him the guts and help him, like the great soft fool you are!

JOSIE: Now don't start raging again, Father.

HOGAN (*Seething*): You've stolen my satchel to give him, I suppose, like you did before for Thomas and John?

JOSIE: It was my satchel, too. Didn't I help you in the trade for the horse, when you got the Crowleys to throw in the satchel for good measure? I was up all night fixing that nag's forelegs so his knees wouldn't buckle together till after the Crowleys had him a day or two.

HOGAN (*Forgets his anger to grin reminiscently*): You've a wonderful way with animals, God bless you.

And do you remember the two Crowleys came back to give me a beating, and I licked them both?

JOSIE (*With calculating flattery*): You did. You're a wonderful fighter. Sure, you could give Jack Dempsey himself a run for his money.

HOGAN (*With sharp suspicion*): I could, but don't try to change the subject and fill me with blarney.

JOSIE: All right. I'll tell the truth then. They were getting the best of you till I ran out and knocked one of them tail over tin cup against the pigpen.

HOGAN (*Outraged*): You're a liar! They was begging for mercy before you came. (*Furiously*): You thief, you! You stole my fine satchel for that lump! And I'll bet that's not all. I'll bet, like when Thomas and John sneaked off, you— (*He rises from the boulder threateningly.*) Listen, Josie, if you found where I hid my little green bag, and stole my money to give to that lousy altar boy, I'll—

JOSIE (*Rises from the steps with the broom handle in her right hand*): Well, I did. So now what'll you do? Don't be threatening me. You know I'll beat better sense in your skull if you lay a finger on me.

HOGAN: I never yet laid hands on a woman—not when I was sober—but if it wasn't for that club— (*Bitterly*): A fine curse God put on me when he gave me a daughter as big and strong as a bull, and as vicious and disrespectful. (*Suddenly his eyes twinkle and he grins admiringly.*) Be God, look at you standing there with the club! If you ain't the damnedest daughter in Connecticut, who is? (*He chuckles and sits on the boulder again.*)

JOSIE (*Laughs and sits on the steps, putting the club away*): And if you ain't the damnedest father in Connecticut, who is?

FROM Fashion

By ANNA CORA MOWATT

Generally regarded as America's very first
satiric comedy of manners, *Fashion* man-
aged to take as its targets a number of types
that are regarded today as still being worthy
of satire. In fact, these "types" present actors
with a problem: how to avoid playing them
in a trite or over-obvious manner. For all
that they are types, they are also individuals,
and must be characterized as such to be
enjoyable to an audience.

(*Enter* MRS. TIFFANY, *followed by* MR. TIFFANY.)

TIFFANY: Your extravagance will ruin me, Mrs.
Tiffany!

MRS. TIFFANY: And your stinginess will ruin me,
Mr. Tiffany! It is totally and *toot a fate* impossible to
convince you of the necessity of keeping up appear-
ances. There is a certain display which every woman
of fashion is forced to make!

TIFFANY: And pray who made *you* a woman of
fashion?

Mrs. Tiffany: What a vulgar question. All women of fashion, Mr. Tiffany—

Tiffany: In this land are self-constituted, like you, Madam—and fashion is the cloak for more sins than charity ever covered! It was for fashion's sake that you insisted upon my purchasing this expensive house—it was for fashion's sake that you ran me in debt at every exorbitant upholsterer's and extravagant furniture warehouse in the city—it was for fashion's sake that you built that ruinous conservatory—hired more servants than they have persons to wait upon—and dressed your footman like a harlequin!

Mrs. Tiffany: Mr. Tiffany, you are thoroughly plebeian, and insufferably American, in your groveling ideas! And, pray, what was the occasion of these very *mal-ap-prop-pos* remarks? Merely because I requested fifty dollars to purchase a new style of head-dress—a *bijou* of an article just introduced in France.

Tiffany: Time was, Mrs. Tiffany, when you manufactured your own French head-dresses—took off their first gloss at the public balls, and then sold them to your shortest-sighted customers. All you knew about France, or French either, was what you spelt out at the bottom of your fashion plates—but now you have grown so fashionable, forsooth, that you have forgotten how to speak your mother tongue!

Mrs. Tiffany: Mr. Tiffany, Mr. Tiffany! Nothing is more positively vulgarian—more unaristocratic than any allusion to the past!

TIFFANY: Why, I thought, my dear, that aristocrats lived principally upon the past—and traded in the market of fashion with the bones of their ancestors for capital.

MRS. TIFFANY: Mr. Tiffany, such vulgar remarks are only suitable to the counting house, in my drawing-room you should—

TIFFANY: Vary my sentiments with my locality, as you change your manners with your dress!

MRS. TIFFANY: Mr. Tiffany, I desire that you will purchase Count d'Orsay's *Science of Etiquette*, and learn how to conduct yourself—especially before you appear at the grand ball, which I shall give on Friday.

TIFFANY: Confound your balls, Madam; they make footballs of my money, while you dance away all that I am worth! A pretty time to give a ball when you know that I am on the very brink of bankruptcy!

MRS. TIFFANY: So much the greater reason that nobody should suspect your circumstances, or you would lose your credit at once. Just at this crisis a ball is absolutely *necessary* to save your reputation! There is Mrs. Adolphus Dashaway—she gave the most splendid fête of the season—and I hear on very good authority that her husband has not paid his baker's bill in three months. Then there was Mrs. Honeywood—

TIFFANY: Gave a ball the night before her husband shot himself—perhaps you wish to drive me to follow his example?

MRS. TIFFANY: Good gracious! Mr. Tiffany, how you talk! I beg you won't mention anything of the kind. I consider black the most unbecoming color. I'm sure I've done all that I could to gratify you. There is that vulgar old torment, Trueman, who gives one the lie fifty times a day—haven't I been very civil to him?

TIFFANY: Civil to his *wealth*, Mrs. Tiffany! I told you that he was a rich, old farmer—the early friend of my father—my own benefactor—and that I had reason to think he might assist me in my present embarrassments. Your civility was *bought*—and like most of your *own* purchases has yet to be paid for.

MRS. TIFFANY: And will be, no doubt! The condescension of a woman of fashion should command any price. Mr. Trueman is insupportably indecorous— he has insulted Count Jolimaitre in the most outrageous manner. If the Count was not so deeply interested—so *abîmé* with Seraphina, I am sure he would never honor us by his visits again!

TIFFANY: So much the better—he shall never marry my daughter!—I am resolved on that. Why, Madam, I am told there is in Paris a regular matrimonial stock company, who fit out indigent dandies for this market. How do I know but this fellow is one of its creatures, and that he has come here to increase its dividends by marrying a fortune?

MRS. TIFFANY: Nonsense, Mr. Tiffany. The Count, the most fashionable young man in all New York— the intimate friend of all the dukes and lords in Europe—not marry my daughter? Not permit Seraphina to become a Countess? Mr. Tiffany, you are out of your senses!

TIFFANY: That would not be very wonderful, considering how many years I have been united to you, my dear. Modern physicians pronounce lunacy infectious!

FROM # Orpheus Descending

By TENNESSEE WILLIAMS

Most of the characters in the dramas of Williams are haunted by inexpressible yearnings, and are doomed never to have their yearnings fulfilled. The man and woman in this scene from one of Williams' less well known plays may be considered typical in this respect. But there is more to them than mere yearning; they are both arresting personalities—odd, unique, not altogether sympathetic, but at the same time magnetically appealing to one another, and to us, the audience.

The scene below comprises the opening of Act II, Scene 1, and it continues in the play for some twenty-five additional speeches beyond what is given here. All of Act I, Scene 2, is a dialogue between the same characters; and there is yet another good scene for a man and woman in the first encounter of Val and Carol in Act I.

This scene takes place in the combination drygoods store-soda shop run by Lady.

Lady is hanging up the phone. Val is standing just outside the door. He turns and enters.

VAL (*Moving to right window*): One a them big Diamond T trucks an' trailors gone off the highway last night and a six mule team is tryin' t' pull it back on.... (*He looks out window.*)

LADY (*Coming from behind to right of counter*): Mister, we just now gotten a big fat complaint about you from a woman that says if she wasn't a widow her husband would come in here and beat the tar out of you.

VAL (*Taking a step toward her*): Yeah? —Is this a small pink-headed woman?

LADY: *Pin*-headed woman did you say?

VAL: Naw, I said, "Pink!" —A little pink-haired woman, in a checkered coat with pearl buttons this big on it.

LADY: I talked to her on the phone. She didn't go into such details about her appearance but she did say you got familiar. I said, "How? by his talk or behavior?" And she said, "Both!" —Now I was afraid of this when I warned you last week, "No monkey business here, boy!"

VAL: This little pink-haired woman bought a valentine from me and all I said is my *name* is Valentine to her. Few minutes later a small colored boy come

in and delivered the valentine to me with something
wrote on it an' I believe I still got it. . . .
(*Finds and shows it to* LADY *who goes to him.* LADY
*reads it, and tears it fiercely to pieces. He lights a
cigarette.*)

LADY: Signed it with a lipstick kiss? You didn't
show up for this date?

VAL: No ma'am. That's why she complained.
(*Throws match on floor.*)

LADY: Pick that match up off the floor.

VAL: Are you bucking for sergeant, or something?
(*He throws match out the door with elaborate care.
Her eyes follow his back.* VAL *returns lazily toward
her.*)

LADY: Did you walk around in front of her that
way?

VAL (*At counter*): What way?

LADY: Slew-foot, slew-foot!
(*He regards her closely with good-humored per-
plexity.*)

LADY: Did you stand in front of her like that? That
close? In that, that—*position?*

VAL: What position?

LADY: Ev'rything you do is suggestive!

VAL: Suggestive of what?

LADY: Of what you said you was through with—somethin'—Oh, shoot, you know what I mean. —Why'd 'ya think I give you a plain, dark business suit to work in?

VAL (*Sadly*): Un-hun.... (*Sighs and removes his blue jacket.*)

LADY: Now what're you takin' that off for?

VAL: I'm giving the suit back to you. I'll change my pants in the closet. (*Gives her the jacket and crosses into the alcove.*)

LADY: Hey! I'm sorry! You hear me? I didn't sleep well last night. Hey! I said I'm sorry! You hear me? (*She enters alcove and returns immediately with VAL's guitar and crosses to down right. He follows.*)

VAL: Le' me have my guitar, Lady. You find too many faults with me and I tried to do good.

LADY: I told you I'm sorry. You want me to get down and lick the dust off your shoes?

VAL: Just give me back my guitar.

LADY: I ain't dissatisfied with you. I'm pleased with you, sincerely!

VAL: You sure don't show it.

LADY: My nerves are all shot to pieces. (*Extends hand to him.*) Shake.

VAL: You mean I ain't fired, so I don't have to quit? (*They shake hands like two men. She hands him guitar—then silence falls between them.*)

LADY: You see, we don't know each other, we're, we're—just gettin'—acquainted.

VAL: That's right, like a couple of animals sniffin' around each other. . . .
(*The image embarrasses her. He crosses to counter, leans over and puts guitar behind it.*)

LADY: Well, not exactly like that, but—!

VAL: We don't know each other. How do people get to know each other? I used to think they did it by touch.

LADY: By what?

VAL: By touch, by touchin' each other.

LADY: (*Moving up and sitting on shoe-fitting chair*): Oh, you mean by close—contact!

VAL: But later it seemed like that made them more strangers than ever, uhh, huh, more strangers than ever. . . .

LADY: Then how d'you think they get to know each other?

VAL (*Sitting on counter*): Well, in answer to your last question, I would say this: Nobody ever gets to know *no body!* We're all of us sentenced to solitary confinement inside our own skins for life! You understand me, Lady? —I'm tellin' you it's the truth, we got to face it, we're under a life-long sentence to solitary confinement inside our own lonely skins for as long as we live on this earth!

FROM The Second Man

By S. N. BEHRMAN

The plays of S. N. Behrman, greatly popular in the 1920's and 1930's, remain unsurpassed for wit and urbanity; and if present trends in the American theater continue, it will be a long time before they are challenged by new comedies of manners.

There are but four characters in *The Second Man*, and the play abounds in excellent scenes for student actors. One might particularly recommend for two men the opening scene in Act III between Storey and Austin.

In this scene from Act II, Scene 2, Mrs. Kendall Frayne is waiting for Clark Storey, the writer who is her lover, and whom she is supporting. The doorbell rings. (It is Storey's apartment.)

(KENDALL *goes out into the hallway and returns in a moment followed by* AUSTIN LOWE. *He is in evening-dress. His manner with* KENDALL *at first is embarrassed and hesitant. Gradually, however, she puts him at ease; she has that sort of manner.*)

KENDALL: Storey's dressing. I'm the first one here.

AUSTIN: Monica's not come yet?

KENDALL: No. Cigarette?

AUSTIN: Er—thanks. (*She lights it for him.*) Thanks.

KENDALL: You and I are the only prompt ones.

AUSTIN: Yes....

KENDALL: Do you know what time it is?

AUSTIN (*Looking*): Ten minutes past eleven.

KENDALL: I was here promptly at eleven. Storey hadn't even *begun* to dress.

AUSTIN: He hadn't!

KENDALL: I'm awfully glad you came. It was lonesome. (*She smiles at him.*)

AUSTIN: I—I'm glad I found *you*.

KENDALL: Why do I never see you?

AUSTIN: Er—see me?

KENDALL: Storey talks about you all the time.

You're one of the few people he respects. I always ask him to bring you to my house but you never come.

AUSTIN: I'm in the laboratory such a lot.

KENDALL: I know. Still I do wish you'd come some time—and bring Miss Grey.... (*She notices him staring at* MONICA's *colored scarf which is lying across a chair.*) What is it?

AUSTIN: That scarf.

KENDALL: You know it?

AUSTIN: It's—it's Monica's.

KENDALL: You dined here with her—didn't you?

AUSTIN: Yes. I did.

KENDALL: Well, then—

AUSTIN: She wore it when I left with her.

KENDALL: Didn't you take her home?

AUSTIN: She told me to go home alone—to save time.

KENDALL: Well, she probably ran back to tell Storey something.

AUSTIN (*Bitterly*): She probably did. It must have

taken a long time because—when you came, Storey hadn't even begun to dress.

KENDALL (*After a moment*): I think you can trust Storey.

AUSTIN: Can I?

KENDALL: He told me over the phone—you and Miss Grey are engaged.

AUSTIN: There's something funny about it.

KENDALL: There's something funny about most things.

AUSTIN (*Warming to her*): Mrs. Frayne—

KENDALL: Call me Kendall.

AUSTIN: Thank you. I wonder—I wonder if Storey tells me everything. I mean—about Monica and himself.

KENDALL: Perhaps he doesn't know everything.

AUSTIN: You mean—perhaps he's in love with her and doesn't know it?

KENDALL: Doesn't know it or won't admit it—even to himself. Perhaps. (*There is a pause.*)

AUSTIN (*Abruptly*): Are you going to marry Storey?

KENDALL: I don't know.

AUSTIN (*Naively*): I wish you would.

KENDALL: It would solve your problem, wouldn't it? It might complicate mine.

AUSTIN: I'm not even sure it would solve mine. I wish I hadn't got into this.

KENDALL (*She stops playing*): It's comforting to know that even a scientific genius is not immune. It rather justifies a weak woman—like me.

AUSTIN: It's rotten to be this way. Wondering about everything, suspecting everybody. Why should I care if Monica came back here or not? And yet—I do.

KENDALL (*Slowly*): I care too, Austin. Isn't it—stupid?

AUSTIN: Do you think Monica's in love with Storey?

KENDALL: You want me to tell you she isn't, don't you?

AUSTIN: Sometimes she tells me she loathes him....

KENDALL: That's bad.

AUSTIN: Do you think so?

KENDALL: Wouldn't it be nice if people were like molecules or electrons or whatever you work with? It would be nice for you because you understand all about those things.

AUSTIN: Molecules are mysterious but they're more predictable than Monica. They obey some sort of law.

KENDALL (*Amused and touched by his sincerity*): I think you're charming, Austin.

FROM **A Doll's House**

By HENRIK IBSEN,
translated *By* WILLIAM ARCHER

"The Father of modern drama!" Sometimes we become so overawed by Ibsen's historical importance that we forget what wonderful plays he wrote. *A Doll's House* is filled with eminently "actable" two-person scenes. There are two good ones between Nora and Mrs. Linden; several for Nora and her husband, Helmer; and one between Mrs. Linden and Krogstad. The one given here is one of two between Nora and Krogstad. It is from Act II.

(KROGSTAD *enters the room in a traveling coat and boots.* NORA *goes to him.*)

NORA: Speak softly; my husband is at home.

KROGSTAD: All right. That's nothing to me.

NORA: What do you want?

KROGSTAD: A little information.

NORA: Be quick, then. What is it?

KROGSTAD: You know I have got my dismissal.

NORA: I couldn't prevent it, Mr. Krogstad. I fought for you to the last, but it was of no use.

KROGSTAD: Does your husband care for you so little? He knows what I can bring upon you, and yet he dares—

NORA: How could you think I should tell him?

KROGSTAD: Well, as a matter of fact, I didn't think it. It wasn't like my friend Torvald Helmer to show so much courage—

NORA: Mr. Krogstad, be good enough to speak respectfully of my husband.

KROGSTAD: Certainly, with all due respect. But since you are so anxious to keep the matter secret, I suppose you are a little clearer than yesterday as to what you have done.

NORA: Clearer than you could ever make me.

KROGSTAD: Yes, such a bad lawyer as I—

NORA: What is it you want?

KROGSTAD: Only to see how you are getting on, Mrs. Helmer. I've been thinking about you all day. Even a mere money-lender, a gutter-journalist, a—in short, a creature like me—has a little bit of what people call feeling.

NORA: Then show it; think of my little children.

KROGSTAD: Did you and your husband think of mine? But enough of that. I only wanted to tell you that you needn't take this matter too seriously. I shall not lodge any information for the present.

NORA: No, surely not. I knew you wouldn't.

KROGSTAD: The whole thing can be settled quite amicably. Nobody need know. It can remain among us three.

NORA: My husband must never know.

KROGSTAD: How can you prevent it? Can you pay off the balance?

NORA: No, not at once.

KROGSTAD: Or have you any means of raising the money in the next few days?

NORA: None—that I will make use of.

KROGSTAD: And if you had, it would not help you now. If you offered me ever so much money down, you should not get back your I.O.U.

NORA: Tell me what you want to do with it.

KROGSTAD: I only want to keep it—to have it in my possession. No outsider shall hear anything of it. So, if you have any desperate scheme in your head—

NORA: What if I have?

KROGSTAD: If you should think of leaving your husband and children—

NORA: What if I do?

KROGSTAD: Or if you should think of—something worse—

NORA: How do you know that?

KROGSTAD: Put all that out of your head.

NORA: How did you know what I had in my mind?

KROGSTAD: Most of us think of *that* at first. I thought of it, too; but I hadn't the courage—

NORA (*Tonelessly*): Nor I.

KROGSTAD (*Relieved*): No, one hasn't. You haven't the courage either, have you?

NORA: I haven't, I haven't.

KROGSTAD: Besides, it would be very foolish. —Just one domestic storm, and it's all over. I have a letter in my pocket for your husband—

NORA: Telling him everything?

KROGSTAD: Sparing you as much as possible.

NORA (*Quickly*): He must never read that letter. Tear it up. I will manage to get the money somehow.

KROGSTAD: Pardon me, Mrs. Helmer, but I believe I told you—

NORA: Oh, I'm not talking about the money I owe you. Tell me how much you demand from my husband—I will get it.

KROGSTAD: I demand no money from your husband.

NORA: What *do* you demand, then?

KROGSTAD: I will tell you. I want to regain my footing in the world. I want to rise; and your husband shall help me to do it. For the last eighteen months my record has been spotless; I have been in bitter need all the time; but I was content to fight my way up, step by step. Now, I've been thrust down again, and I will not be satisfied with merely being reinstated as a matter of grace. I want to rise, I tell you. I must get into the Bank again, in a higher position than before. Your husband shall create a place on purpose for me—

NORA: He will never do that!

KROGSTAD: He will do it; I know him—he won't

dare to show fight. And when he and I are together there, you shall soon see! Before a year is out, I shall be the manager's right hand. It won't be Torvald Helmer, but Nils Krogstad, that manages the Joint Stock Bank.

NORA: That shall never be.

KROGSTAD: Perhaps you will—?

NORA: *Now* I have the courage for it.

KROGSTAD: Oh, you don't frighten me! A sensitive, petted creature like you—

NORA: You shall see, you shall see!

KROGSTAD: Under the ice, perhaps? Down into the cold, black water? And next spring to come up again, ugly, hairless, unrecognizable—

NORA: You can't terrify me.

KROGSTAD: Nor you me. People don't do that sort of thing, Mrs. Helmer. And, after all, what would be the use of it? I have your husband in my pocket all the same.

NORA: Afterwards? When I am no longer—?

KROGSTAD: You forget, your reputation remains in my hands. (NORA *stands speechless and looks at him.*)

Well, now you are prepared. Do nothing foolish. As soon as Helmer has received my letter, I shall expect to hear from him. And remember that it is your husband himself who has forced me back again into such paths. That I will never forgive him. Good-bye, Mrs. Helmer. (*He goes out through the hall door.*)

FROM **Cymbeline**

By WILLIAM SHAKESPEARE

With its strange parallels to the children's tale of Snow White and the Seven Dwarfs—including a wicked stepmother of a Queen, a Princess reportedly slain but in actuality hiding in the forest, and the woodland creatures who offer her refuge—it is no wonder that *Cymbeline* is one of Shakespeare's least performed plays. Yet it does deserve to be better known, if for no other reason than that its heroine, Imogen, is one of the most enchanting ingenue roles written by Shakespeare.

The scene given here is Scene 4 from Act III. Pisanio, servant to Imogen's husband, has been ordered to lead the girl into the country and kill her, Imogen's husband having been falsely led to believe that she has been unfaithful to him.

(*Enter* PISANIO *and* IMOGEN.)

IMOGEN: Thou told'st me, when we came from horse, the place
Was near at hand: ne'er long'd my mother so

To see me first, as I have now. Pisanio! man!
Where is Posthumus? What is in thy mind,
That makes thee stare thus? Wherefore breaks that
 sigh
From th'inward of thee? One, but painted thus,
Would be interpreted a thing perplex'd
Beyond self-explication: put thyself
Into a haviour of less fear, ere wildness
Vanquish my staider senses. What's the matter?
Why tender'st thou that paper to me, with
A look untender? If't be summer news,
Smile to 't before; if winterly, thou need'st
But keep that countenance still. My husband's hand!
That drug-damn'd Italy hath out-crafted him,
And he's at some hard point. Speak, man: thy tongue
May take off some extremity, which to read
Would be even mortal to me.

 PISANIO: Please you, read;
And you shall find me, wretched man, a thing
The most disdain'd of fortune.

 IMOGEN (*Reads*): "Thy mistress, Pisanio, hath
played the strumpet in my bed; the testimonies
whereof lie bleeding in me. I speak not out of weak
surmises, but from proof as strong as my grief and
as certain as I expect my revenge. That part thou,
Pisanio, must act for me, if thy faith be not tainted
with the breach of hers. Let thine own hands take
away her life: I shall give thee opportunity at Milford-
Haven. She hath my letter for the purpose: where, if
thou fear to strike and to make me certain it is done,
thou art the pandar to her dishonour and equally to
me disloyal."

PISANIO: What shall I need to draw my sword?
    the paper
Hath cut her throat already. No, 'tis slander,
Whose edge is sharper than the sword, whose tongue
Outvenoms all the worms of Nile, whose breath
Rides on the posting winds and doth belie
All corners of the world: kings, queens and states,
Maids, matrons, nay, the secrets of the grave
This viperous slander enters. What cheer, madam?

IMOGEN: False to his bed! What is it to be false?
To lie in watch there and to think on him?
To weep 'twixt clock and clock? if sleep charge nature,
To break it with a fearful dream of him
And cry myself awake? that's false to's bed, is it?

PISANIO: Alas, good lady!

IMOGEN: I false! Thy conscience witness: Iachimo,
Thou didst accuse him of incontinency;
Thou then look'dst like a villain; now methinks
Thy favour's good enough. Some jay of Italy
Whose mother was her painting, hath betray'd him:
Poor I am stale, a garment out of fashion;
And, for I am richer than to hang by the walls,
I must be ripp'd: —to pieces with me!— O,
Men's vows are women's traitors! All good seeming,
By thy revolt, O husband, shall be thought
Put on for villainy; not born where't grows,
But worn a bait for ladies.

PISANIO: Good madam, hear me.

IMOGEN: True honest men being heard, like false
    Aeneas,
Were in his time thought false, and Sinon's weeping
Did scandal many a holy tear, took pity
From most true wretchedness: so thou, Posthumus,
Wilt lay the leaven on all proper men;
Goodly and gallant shall be false and perjured
From thy great fail. Come, fellow, be thou honest:
Do thou thy master's bidding: when thou see'st him,
A little witness my obedience: look!
I draw the sword myself: take it, and hit
The innocent mansion of my love, my heart:
Fear not; 'tis empty of all things but grief:
Thy master is not there, who was indeed
The riches of it: do his bidding; strike.
Thou mayst be valiant in a better cause;
But now thou seem'st a coward.

PISANIO: Hence, vile instrument!
Thou shalt not damn my hand.

IMOGEN: Why, I must die;
And if I do not by thy hand, thou art
No servant of thy master's. Against self-slaughter
There is a prohibition so divine
That cravens my weak hand. Come, here's my heart.
Something's afore't. Soft, soft! we'll no defence;
Obedient as the scabbard. What is here?
The scriptures of the loyal Leonatus,
All turn'd to heresy? Away, away,
Corrupters of my faith! you shall no more
Be stomachers to my heart. Thus may poor fools
Believe false teachers: though those that are betray'd

Do feel the treason sharply, yet the traitor
Stands in worse case of woe.
And thou, Posthumus, thou that didst set up
My disobedience 'gainst the king my father
And make me put into contempt the suits
Of princely fellows, shalt hereafter find
It is no act of common passage, but
A strain of rareness: and I grieve myself
To think, when thou shalt be disedged by her
That now thou tirest on, how thy memory
Will then be pang'd by me. Prithee, dispatch:
The lamb entreats the butcher: where's thy knife?
Thou art too slow to do thy master's bidding,
When I desire it too.

PISANIO: O gracious lady,
Since I received command to do this business
I have not slept one wink.

IMOGEN: Do't, and to bed then.

PISANIO: I'll wake mine eyeballs blind first.

IMOGEN: Wherefore then
Didst undertake it? Why hast thou abused
So many miles with a pretence? this place?
Mine action and thine own? our horses' labour?
The time inviting thee? the perturb'd court,
For my being absent? whereunto I never
Purpose return. Why hast thou gone so far,
To be unbent when thou hast ta'en thy stand,
The elected deer before thee?

PISANIO: But to win time

To lose so bad employment; in the which
I have consider'd of a course. Good lady,
Hear me with patience.

IMOGEN: Talk thy tongue weary; speak:
I have heard I am a strumpet; and mine ear,
Therein false struck, can take no greater wound,
Nor tent to bottom that. But speak.

PISANIO: Then, madam,
I thought you would not back again.

IMOGEN: Most like;
Bringing me here to kill me.

PISANIO: Not so, neither:
But if I were as wise as honest, then
My purpose would prove well. It cannot be
But that my master is abused:
Some villain, ay, and singular in his art,
Hath done you both this cursed injury.

IMOGEN: Some Roman courtezan.

PISANIO: No, on my life.
I'll give but notice you are dead and send him
Some bloody sign of it; for 'tis commanded
I should do so: you shall be miss'd at court,
And that will well confirm it.

IMOGEN: Why, good fellow,
What shall I do the while? where bide? how live?
Or in my life what comfort, when I am
Dead to my husband?

PISANIO: If you'll back to the court—

IMOGEN: No court, no father; nor no more ado
With that harsh, noble, simple nothing,
That Cloten, whose love-suit hath been to me
As fearful as a siege.

PISANIO: If not at court,
Then not in Britain must you bide.

IMOGEN: Where then?
Hath Britain all the sun that shines? Day, night,
Are they not but in Britain? I' the world's volume
Our Britain seems as of it, but not in't;
In a great pool a swan's nest: prithee, think
There's livers out of Britain.

PISANIO: I am most glad
You think of other place. The ambassador,
Lucius the Roman, comes to Milford-Haven
To-morrow: now, if you could wear a mind
Dark as your fortune is, and but disguise
That which, to appear itself, must not yet be
But by self-danger, you should tread a course
Pretty and full of view; yea, haply, near
The residence of Posthumus; so nigh at least
That though his actions were not visible, yet
Report should render him hourly to your ear
As truly as he moves.

IMOGEN: O, for such means!
Though peril to my modesty, not death on't,
I would adventure.

PISANIO: Well, then, here's the point:
You must forget to be a woman; change
Command into obedience: fear and niceness—
The handmaids of all women, or, more truly,
Woman its pretty self—into a waggish courage;
Ready in gibes, quick-answer'd, saucy and
As quarrelous as the weasel; nay, you must
Forget the rarest treasure of your cheek,
Exposing it—but, O, the harder heart!
Alack, no remedy!—to the greedy touch
Of common-kissing Titan, and forget
Your laboursome and dainty trims, wherein
You made great Juno angry.

IMOGEN: Nay, be brief:
I see into thy end, and am almost
A man already.

PISANIO: First, make yourself but like one.
Fore-thinking this, I have already fit—
'Tis in my cloak-bag—doublet, hat, hose, all
That answer to them: would you in their serving,
And with what imitation you can borrow
From youth of such a season, 'fore noble Lucius
Present yourself, desire his service, tell him
Wherein you're happy, —which you'll make him know,
If that his head have ear in music, —doubtless
With joy he will embrace you, for he's honourable
And doubling that, most holy. Your means abroad,
You have me, rich; and I will never fail
Beginning nor supplyment.

IMOGEN: Thou art all the comfort
The gods will diet me with. Prithee, away:

There's more to be consider'd; but we'll even
All that good time will give us: this attempt
I am soldier to, and will abide it with
A prince's courage. Away, I prithee.

PISANIO: Well, madam, we must take a short fare-
    well,
Lest, being miss'd, I be suspected of
Your carriage from the court. My noble mistress,
Here is a box; I had it from the queen:
What's in't is precious; if you are sick at sea,
Or stomach-qualm'd at land, a dram of this
Will drive away distemper. To some shade,
And fit you to your manhood. May the gods
Direct you to the best!

IMOGEN: Amen: I thank thee.
(*Exeunt, severally.*)

The Circle

By W. SOMERSET MAUGHAM

What the comedies of Behrman are to the American stage, the comedies of Maugham are to the British: urbane, polished, witty, but genuinely human.

The Circle has a number of choice scenes for one actor and one actress. In addition to the one given here, there are those in Act III between Elizabeth and Teddie, and between Porteous and Lady Kitty.

This scene is from Act II. It is between Elizabeth and Arnold, young wife and somewhat older husband. As this is a true British comedy of manners, the action passes in the stately Georgian drawing room of a gracious country residence.

ARNOLD (*Entering*): Hulloa! Oh, Elizabeth, I've found an illustration here of a chair which is almost identical with mine. It's dated 1750. Look!

ELIZABETH: That's very interesting.

ARNOLD: I want to show it to Porteous. (*Moving a chair which has been misplaced*): You know, it does exasperate me the way people will not leave things alone. I no sooner put a thing in its place than somebody moves it.

ELIZABETH: It must be maddening for you.

ARNOLD: It is. You are the worst offender. I can't think why you don't take the pride that I do in the house. After all, it's one of the show places in the country.

ELIZABETH: I'm afraid you find me very unsatisfactory.

ARNOLD (*Good-humoredly*): I don't know about that. But my two subjects are politics and decoration. I should be a perfect fool if I didn't see that you don't care two straws about either.

ELIZABETH: We haven't much in common, Arnold, have we?

ARNOLD: I don't think you can blame me for that.

ELIZABETH: I don't. I blame you for nothing. I have no fault to find with you.

ARNOLD (*Surprised at her significant tone*): Good gracious me! What's the meaning of all this?

ELIZABETH: Well, I don't think there's any object in beating about the bush. I want you to let me go.

ARNOLD: Go where?

ELIZABETH: Away. For always.

ARNOLD: My dear child, what *are* you talking about?

ELIZABETH: I want to be free.

ARNOLD (*Amused rather than disconcerted*): Don't be ridiculous, darling. I daresay you're run down and want a change. I'll take you over to Paris for a fortnight if you like.

ELIZABETH: I shouldn't have spoken to you if I hadn't quite made up my mind. We've been married for three years and I don't think it's been a great success. I'm frankly bored by the life you want me to lead.

ARNOLD: Well, if you'll allow me to say so, the fault is yours. We lead a very distinguished, useful life. We know a lot of extremely nice people.

ELIZABETH: I'm quite willing to allow that the fault is mine. But how does that make it any better? I'm only twenty-five. If I've made a mistake I have time to correct it.

ARNOLD: I can't bring myself to take you very seriously.

ELIZABETH: You see, I don't love you.

ARNOLD: Well, I'm awfully sorry. But you weren't obliged to marry me. You've made your bed and I'm afraid you must lie on it.

ELIZABETH: That's one of the falsest proverbs in the English language. Why should you lie on the bed you've made if you don't want to? There's always the floor.

ARNOLD: For goodness' sake don't be funny, Elizabeth.

ELIZABETH: I've quite made up my mind to leave you, Arnold.

ARNOLD: Come, come, Elizabeth, you must be sensible. You haven't any reason to leave me.

ELIZABETH: Why should you wish to keep a woman tied to you who wants to be free?

ARNOLD: I happen to be in love with you.

ELIZABETH: You might have said that before.

ARNOLD: I thought you'd take it for granted. You can't expect a man to go on making love to his wife after three years. I'm very busy. I'm awfully keen on politics and I've worked like a dog to make this house a thing of beauty. After all, a man marries to have a home, but also because he doesn't want to be bothered with sex and all that sort of thing. I fell in love with you the first time I saw you and I've been in love ever since.

ELIZABETH: I'm sorry, but if you're not in love with a man his love doesn't mean very much to you.

ARNOLD: It's so ungrateful. I've done everything in the world for you.

ELIZABETH: You've been very kind to me. But you've asked me to lead a life I don't like and that I'm not suited for. I'm awfully sorry to cause you pain, but now you must let me go.

ARNOLD: Nonsense! I'm a good deal older than you are and I think I have a little more sense. In your interests as well as in mine I'm not going to do anything of the sort.

ELIZABETH (*With a smile*): How can you prevent me? You can't keep me under lock and key.

ARNOLD: Please don't talk to me as if I were a foolish child. You're my wife and you're going to remain my wife.

ELIZABETH: What sort of a life do you think we should lead? Do you think there'd be any more happiness for you than for me?

ARNOLD: But what is it precisely that you suggest?

ELIZABETH: Well, I want you to let me divorce you.

ARNOLD (*Astounded*): Me? Thank you very much. Are you under the impression I'm going to sacrifice my career for a whim of yours?

ELIZABETH: How will it do that?

ARNOLD: My seat's wobbly enough as it is. Do you think I'd be able to hold it if I were in a divorce case? Even if it were a put-up job, as most divorces are nowadays, it would damn me.

ELIZABETH: It's rather hard on a woman to be divorced.

ARNOLD (*With sudden suspicion*): What do you mean by that? Are you in love with some one?

ELIZABETH: Yes.

ARNOLD: Who?

ELIZABETH: Teddie Luton.
(*He is astonished for a moment, then bursts into a laugh.*)

ARNOLD: My poor child, how can you be so ridiculous? Why, he hasn't a bob. He's a perfectly commonplace young man. It's so absurd I can't even be angry with you.

ELIZABETH: I've fallen desperately in love with him, Arnold.

ARNOLD: Well, you'd better fall desperately out.

ELIZABETH: He wants to marry me.

ARNOLD: I daresay he does. He can go to hell.

ELIZABETH: It's no good talking like that.

ARNOLD: Is he your lover?

ELIZABETH: No, certainly not.

ARNOLD: It shows that he's a mean skunk to take advantage of my hospitality to make love to you.

ELIZABETH: He's never even kissed me.

ARNOLD: I'd try telling that to the horse marines if I were you.

ELIZABETH: It's because I wanted to do nothing shabby that I told you straight out how things were.

ARNOLD: How long have you been thinking of this?

ELIZABETH: I've been in love with Teddie ever since I knew him.

ARNOLD: And you never thought of me at all, I suppose?

ELIZABETH: Oh, yes, I did. I was miserable. But I can't help myself. I wish I loved you, but I don't.

ARNOLD: I recommend you to think very carefully before you do anything foolish.

ELIZABETH: I have thought very carefully.

ARNOLD: By God! I don't know why I don't give you a sound hiding. I'm not sure if that wouldn't be the best thing to bring you to your senses.

ELIZABETH: Oh, Arnold, don't take it like that.

ARNOLD: How do you expect me to take it! You come to me quite calmly and say: "I've had enough of you. We've been married three years and I think I'd like to marry somebody else now. Shall I break up your home? What a bore for you! Do you mind my divorcing you? It'll smash up your career, will it? What a pity!" Oh, no, my girl, I may be a fool, but I'm not a damned fool!

FROM Uncle Vanya

By ANTON CHEKOV

Though he wrote only five major full-length plays, Chekov's influence on the entire body of world dramatic literature that followed him was profound. In his plays, interior action takes precedence over exterior action; the subtext—what the characters are really thinking—is more important than the lines they speak. Critics have accused his plays of being static and talky; they are—when they're improperly acted!

In the scene below, from Act IV of *Uncle Vanya*, the beautiful Yelena, married to a pedant much older than she, takes her farewell of the young, vigorous, intellectual Dr. Astrov. They had contemplated an affair, but it had come to nothing. (Other scenes from the play for one actor and actress are those between these same characters in Act III, between Yelena and her husband at the opening of Act II, and between Astrov and Sonya in Act II. A scene between Sonya and Yelena appears elsewhere in this book.)

YELENA: I am going away. (*Gives* ASTROV *her hand.*) Good-bye.

ASTROV: Already?

YELENA: The carriage is waiting.

ASTROV: Good-bye.

YELENA: You promised me to-day that you would go away.

ASTROV: I remember. I am just going. (*A pause.*) You have taken fright? (*Taking her hand*): Is it so terrible?

YELENA: Yes.

ASTROV: You had better stay, after all! What do you say? To-morrow in the plantation—

YELENA: No. It's settled. And I look at you so fearlessly just because it is settled. I have only one favor to ask of you: think better of me. I should like you to have respect for me.

ASTROV: Ugh! (*Makes a gesture of impatience.*) Do stay, I ask you to. Do recognize, you have nothing to do in this world, you have no object in life, you have nothing to occupy your mind, and sooner or later you will give way to feeling—it's inevitable. And it had better not be at Harkov, or somewhere in Kursk, but here, in the lap of nature.... It's poetical, anyway, even the autumn is beautiful.... There is the forest plantation here, half-ruined homesteads in the Turgenev style....

YELENA: How absurd you are.... I am angry with you, but yet.... I shall think of you with pleasure. You are an interesting, original man. We shall never meet again, and so—why conceal it?—I was really a little bit in love with you. Come, let us shake hands and part friends. Don't remember evil against me.

ASTROV (*Pressing her hand*): Yes, you had better go.... (*Musing*): You seem to be a good, warm-hearted creature, and yet there is something strange about your whole personality, as it were. You came here with your husband, and all of us who were at work, toiling and creating something, had to fling aside our work and attend to nothing all the summer but your husband's gout and you. The two of you have infected all of us with your idleness. I was attracted by you and have done nothing for a whole month, and, meanwhile, people have been ill, and the peasants have pastured their cattle in my woods of young, half-grown trees.... And so, wherever you and your husband go, you bring destruction everywhere.... I am joking, of course, yet...it is strange. And I am convinced that if you had stayed here, the devastation would have been immense. I should have been done for...and you wouldn't have fared well either! Well, go away. *Finita la commedia.*

YELENA (*Taking a pencil from his table and hurriedly putting it in her pocket*): I shall take this pencil as a keepsake.

ASTROV: It's strange.... We have been friends and all at once for some reason...we shall never meet again. So it is with everything in this world.... While there is no one here—before Uncle Vanya comes in with a nosegay—allow me to kiss you at parting.... Yes? (*He kisses her on the cheek.*) That's right.

YELENA: I wish you all happiness. (*Looks around.*) Well, so be it! For once in my life! (*She embraces him impulsively and both simultaneously draw apart from each other.*) I must go—I must go!

ASTROV: Make haste and go. Since the carriage is there, you had better set off.

YELENA: There's someone coming, I believe. (*Both listen.*)

ASTROV: *Finita!*

The Autumn Garden

By LILLIAN HELLMAN

Although she achieved her greatest fame for tightly constructed dramas, in *The Autumn Garden* Lillian Hellman wrote a fine play that was almost Chekovian in its development of many individual characters at the expense of pure story. Yet her skill as a dramatist did not desert her; *The Autumn Garden* is filled with scenes that are an actor's dream. There is probably not her equal for giving actors solid, meaty parts they can "get their teeth into."

Choosing specific two-person scenes for inclusion in this book was no easy matter; *The Autumn Garden* is filled with them. The one below is the final scene in the play. Elsewhere in this collection there is another scene from *The Autumn Garden* for two actresses.

Constance Tuckerman and Ned Crossman are middle-aged Southerners who have known each other from childhood.

CONSTANCE (*After a silence*): I hate this house today.

CROSSMAN: Well, they'll all be gone soon.

CONSTANCE: You won't go? Please.

CROSSMAN: I'll stay for a few days if you'd like me to.

CONSTANCE: Oh, yes. I need you to stay.

CROSSMAN (*Pointing out of window*): Don't worry about what the town thinks. Just act as if nothing had happened and they'll soon stop talking.

CONSTANCE: Oh, I'm not worrying about that. (*Pauses.*) I feel so lost, Ned. As if I distrusted myself, didn't have anything to stand on. I mean, right now, if you asked me, I just wouldn't know what I thought or believed, or ever had, or— (*Shyly*): Well, what *have* I built my life on? Do you know what I mean?

CROSSMAN: Sure. I know.

CONSTANCE (*As if she had trouble with the words*): It's—it's so painful. (*Then, as if she wished to change the subject quickly*): Sophie will be going back to Europe. She just told me. She *wants* to go. Did you know that?

CROSSMAN: Is that so?

CONSTANCE: I was so sure I was doing the right

thing, bringing her here. You see? That's part of what I mean by not knowing the things I thought I knew. Well. She wants me to come with her and live with them, but I told her I'd be no happier in a new life than she was. (*Pauses, as if she were coming to something that frightens her.*) Nick said you wouldn't be coming here next summer. Did you say anything like that, or was it one of Nick's lies? (*He does not answer her. She stares at him.*) Why, Ned?

CROSSMAN: Hasn't anything to do with you, Con. Just think I'd be better off. You know, it's kind of foolish—two weeks a year—coming back here and living a life that isn't me any more. (*Laughs.*) It's too respectable for me, Con. I ain't up to it any more.

CONSTANCE: Oh. It's what I look forward to every summer. What will I— (*Very quickly*): Where is Nick? I haven't seen him. I wish they'd leave—

CROSSMAN: They've gone.

CONSTANCE (*Staring at him*): Without a word to me? Exactly the way he left years ago. I didn't ever tell you that, did I? We had a date for dinner. He didn't come. He just got on the boat. I didn't ever tell anybody before. (*Violently*): What a fool. All these years of making a shabby man into the kind of hero who would come back some day all happy and shining—

CROSSMAN: Oh, don't do that. He never asked you to make him what he wasn't. Or to wait twenty years to find him out.

CONSTANCE: No, he didn't. That's true.
(*She rises, goes to the portrait and stands staring at it.*)

CONSTANCE: Do I look like this?

CROSSMAN: You look nice.

CONSTANCE: Come and look at it.

CROSSMAN: No. I don't want to.

CONSTANCE: Much older than I thought or— And I don't look very bright. (*She puts the picture away from her.*)

CONSTANCE: Well, I haven't been very bright. I want to say something to you. I can't wait any longer. Would you forgive me?

CROSSMAN: Forgive you? For what?

CONSTANCE: For wasting all these years. For not knowing what I felt about you, or not wanting to. Ned, would you have me now?

CROSSMAN: (*After a second*): What did you say?

CONSTANCE: Would you marry me?
(*There is a pause. Offstage, we hear* SOPHIE *singing a cheerful French song.* CONSTANCE *smiles.*)

CONSTANCE: She's happy. That's good. I think she'll come out all right, always!

CROSSMAN (*Stares at* CONSTANCE, *then slowly, carefully*): I live in a room and I go to work and I play a game called getting through the day while you wait for night. The night's for me—just me—and I can do anything with it I want. There used to be a lot of things to do with it, good things, but now there's a bar and another bar and the same people in each bar. When I've had enough I go back to my room—or somebody else's room—and that never means much one way or the other. A few years ago I'd have weeks of reading—night after night—just me. But I don't do that much any more. Just read, all night long. You can feel good that way.

CONSTANCE: I never did that. I'm not a reader.

CROSSMAN (*As if he hadn't heard her*): And a few years ago I'd go on the wagon twice a year. Now I don't do that anymore. And I don't care. (*Smiles.*) And all these years I told myself that if you'd loved me everything would have been different. I'd have had a good life, been worth something to myself. I wanted to believe it. Griggs was right. I not only wasted myself, but I wanted it that way. All my life, I guess, I wanted it that way.

CONSTANCE: And you're not in love with me, Ned?

CROSSMAN: No, Con. Not now.

CONSTANCE: (*Gets up, goes to him*): Let's have a nice dinner together, just you and me, and go to the movies. Could we do that?

CROSSMAN: I've kept myself busy looking into other people's hearts so I wouldn't have to look into my own. (*Softly*): If I made you think I was still in love, I'm sorry. Sorry I fooled you and sorry I fooled myself. And I've never liked liars—least of all those who lie to themselves.

CONSTANCE: Never mind. Most of us lie to ourselves, darling, most of us. (*The curtain falls.*)

FROM Patience

By W. S. GILBERT

The conventions of acting in a play with music vary a good deal from those of the straight play; and when the world of the play is as special as that in Gilbert & Sullivan's *Patience*, actors need a great deal of skill indeed if they are to be bearable, much less believable. This scene, therefore, is a real test of ability to play with style.

Grosvenor is a beautiful young poet; Patience is a winsome dairymaid. Both of them are Innocence personified.

GROSVENOR: Patience! Can it be that you don't recognize me?

PATIENCE: Recognize you? Indeed I don't!

GROSVENOR: Have fifteen years so greatly changed me?

PATIENCE: Fifteen years? What do you mean?

GROSVENOR: Have you forgotten the friend of your youth, your Archibald? —your little playfellow? Oh,

Chronos, Chronos, this is too bad of you!

PATIENCE: Archibald! Is it possible? Why, let me look! It is! It is! It must be! Oh, how happy I am! I thought we should never meet again! And how you've grown!

GROSVENOR: Yes, Patience, I am much taller and much stouter than I was.

PATIENCE: And how you've improved!

GROSVENOR: Yes, Patience, I am very beautiful! (Sighs.)

PATIENCE: But surely *that* doesn't make you unhappy.

GROSVENOR: Yes, Patience. Gifted as I am with a beauty which probably has not its rival on earth, I am, nevertheless, utterly and completely miserable.

PATIENCE: Oh—but why?

GROSVENOR: My child-love for you has never faded. Conceive, then, the horror of my situation when I tell you that it is my hideous destiny to be madly loved at first sight by every woman I come across!

PATIENCE: But why do you make yourself so picturesque? Why not disguise yourself, disfigure yourself, anything to escape this persecution?

GROSVENOR: No, Patience, that may not be. These

gifts—irksome as they are—were given to me for the enjoyment and delectation of my fellow-creatures. I am a trustee for Beauty, and it is my duty to see that the conditions of my trust are faithfully discharged.

PATIENCE: And you, too, are a Poet?

GROSVENOR: Yes, I am the Apostle of Simplicity. I am called "Archibald the All-Right"—for I am infallible!

PATIENCE: And is it possible that you condescend to love such a girl as I?

GROSVENOR: Yes, Patience, is it not strange? I have loved you with a Florentine fourteenth-century frenzy for full fifteen years!

PATIENCE: Oh, marvellous! I have hitherto been deaf to the voice of love. I seem now to know what love is! It has been revealed to me—it is Archibald Grosvenor!

GROSVENOR: Yes, Patience, it is!

PATIENCE (*As in a trance*): We will never, never part!

GROSVENOR: We will live and die together!

PATIENCE: I swear it!

GROSVENOR: We both swear it!

PATIENCE (*Recoiling from him*): But—oh, horror!

GROSVENOR: What's the matter?

PATIENCE: Why, you are perfection! A source of endless ecstasy to all who know you!

GROSVENOR: I know I am. Well?

PATIENCE: Then, bless my heart, there can be nothing unselfish in loving *you!*

GROSVENOR: Merciful powers! I never thought of that!

PATIENCE: To monopolize those features on which all women love to linger! It would be unpardonable!

GROSVENOR: Why, so it would! Oh, fatal perfection, again you interpose between me and my happiness!

PATIENCE: Oh, if you were but a thought less beautiful than you are!

GROSVENOR: Would that I were; but candour compels me to admit that I'm not!

PATIENCE: Our duty is clear; we must part, and for ever!

GROSVENOR: Oh, misery! And yet I cannot question the propriety of your decision. Farewell, Patience!

PATIENCE: Farewell, Archibald! But stay!

GROSVENOR: Yes, Patience?

PATIENCE: Although I may not love *you*—for you are perfection—there is nothing to prevent your loving *me*. I am plain, homely, unattractive!

GROSVENOR: Why, that's true!

PATIENCE: The love of such a man as you for such a girl as I must be unselfish!

GROSVENOR: Unselfishness itself!

FROM **Secret Service**

By WILLIAM GILLETTE

The young lovers in *Secret Service* bear a
striking resemblance to those in *Patience*,
although the one is a murky melodrama
and the other a light comic opera. In this
case, however, the stiltedness and artificial-
ity of the characters was not deliberate; and
it is therefore imperative that the actors
playing them believe implicitly in their
reality.

The action takes place during the 'American Civil War. Caroline Mitford and Wilfred
Varney enter the room from side doors on
either side of the stage, and start for the
main door up center when they meet.

CAROLINE (*After a pause*): Good evening... (*with
emphasis*) Mr. Varney!

WILFRED (*Coldly*): Good evening... (*with emphasis*) Miss Mitford! (*Both start rapidly toward
door, but, as it brings them toward each other, stop
simultaneously in order to avoid meeting in the
doorway.*)

CAROLINE: Excuse me—I'm in a *great* hurry!

WILFRED: That's plain enough! (*Contemptuously*): Another party, I reckon.

CAROLINE: You reckon perfectly correctly—it *is* another party!

WILFRED: Dancing!

CAROLINE: Well—what of it? What's the matter with dancing, I'd like to know!

WILFRED: Nothing's the matter with it—if you want to *do* it!

CAROLINE: Well, I want to *do* it fast enough, if that's all you mean!

WILFRED: But I must say it's a pretty way to carry on—with the sound of the cannon not six miles away!

CAROLINE: Well, what do you want us to do—sit down and cry about it? A heap o' good *that* would do now, wouldn't it?

WILFRED: Oh—I haven't time to talk about it. (*Turns as if to go.*)

CAROLINE: Well it was you who started *out* to talk about it—I'm right sure *I* didn't!

WILFRED (*Stops dead on* CAROLINE's *speech, and, after a quick glance to see that no one is near, goes to her*): You needn't try to fool me! I know well enough how you've been carrying on since our engagement was broken off! Half a dozen officers proposing to you—a dozen, for all I know!

CAROLINE: What difference does it make? I haven't got to *marry* 'em, have I?

WILFRED: Well—it isn't very nice to go on like that I must say—proposals by the wholesale! (*Turns away.*)

CAROLINE: Goodness gracious—what's the use of talking to me about it? *They're* the ones that propose—*I* don't!

WILFRED (*Turning on her*): Well, what do you let 'em *do* it for?

CAROLINE: How can I help it?

WILFRED (*Sneering*): Ho! Any girl can help it! You helped it with *me* all right!

CAROLINE (*Glancing oddly at the floor*): Well—that was different!

WILFRED: And ever since you threw me ovah—

CAROLINE (*Looking up at him indignantly*): Oh! I *didn't* throw you ovah—you just *went* ovah!

WILFRED: Well, I went over because you walked off alone with Major Sillsby that night we were at Drury's Bluff an' encouraged him to propose— (CARO-

LINE *looks round in wrath.*) Yes—(*advancing*): *En-couraged* him!

CAROLINE: Of *co'se* I did! I didn't want 'im hangin' round forever, did I? That's the on'y way to finish 'em off!

WILFRED: You want to finish too many of 'em off! Nearly every officer in the Seventeenth Virginyah, I'll be sworn!

CAROLINE: Well, what do you want me to do—string a placard around my neck saying, "No proposals received here—apply at the office!" Would that make you feel any better?

WILFRED (*Throwing it off with pretended casualness*): Oh—it doesn't make any difference to me what you do!

CAROLINE: Well, if it doesn't make any difference to you, it doesn't even make as much as that to me! (*Turns and goes to couch; sits on left end of it.*)

WILFRED (*Turning on her again*): Oh—it doesn't! I think it *does*, though! You looked as if you enjoyed it pretty well while the Third Virginyah was in the city!

CAROLINE (*Jumping to her feet*): Enjoyed it! I should think I did! I just love every one of 'em! They're on their way to the front! They're going to fight for us—an'—an' die for us—an' I *love* 'em!

WILFRED: Well, why don't you accept one of 'em an' be done with it!

CAROLINE: How do you know but what I'm going to?

WILFRED (*Goes to her a little*): I suppose it'll be one of those *smart* young fellows with a cavalry uniform!

CAROLINE: It'll be *some* kind of uniform, I can tell you that! It won't be anybody that stays here in Richmond!

WILFRED (*Unable to say anything for a few seconds, looks about room helplessly, and then speaks in a low voice*): Now I see what it was! I had to stay in Richmond—an' so you—an' so—

CAROLINE (*Looking down, playing with something with her foot*): Well, that made a heap o' difference! (*Looks up; different tone*): Why, I was the on'y girl on Franklin Street that didn't have a—a—(*hesitates*) —someone she was engaged to at the front! The on'y one! Just *think* what it was to be out of it like that! Why, you've no idea what I suffered! Besides, it's our—it's our *duty* to help all we can!

WILFRED: Help!

CAROLINE: Yes—help! There aren't many things we girls can do—I know that well enough! But Colonel Woodbridge—he's one o' Morgan's men, you know— well, he told Mollie Pickens that the boys fight *twice* as well when they have a—a sweetheart at home!

WILFRED (*Glances quickly about as he thinks*): He said *that*, did he!

CAROLINE: Yes—an' if we can make 'em fight twice as well, why, we just ought to do it, that's all! We girls can't do much, but we can do *something!*

WILFRED (*Short pause; he makes an absent-minded motion of feeling the package under his arm*): You're in earnest, are you?

CAROLINE: Earnest!

WILFRED: You really want to help—all you can?

CAROLINE: Well, I should think I *did!*

WILFRED: Yes—but do you *now?*

CAROLINE: Of co'se—that's what I say!

WILFRED: An' if I was— (*Glances around cautiously.*) If I was going to join the army—would you help *me?*

CAROLINE (*Looking down in slight embarrassment*): Why, of co'se I would—if it was anything I could do!

WILFRED (*Earnestly, quite near her*): Oh, it's something you can *do*, all right!

CAROLINE (*Hardly daring to look up*): What is it?

WILFRED (*Unrolling a pair of old gray army trousers, taking them from under his coat so that they unfurl before her*): Cut these off! (*Short pause.*

CAROLINE *looks at trousers.* WILFRED *soon goes on very earnestly, holding trousers before his own legs to measure*): They're about twice too long! All you got to do is to cut 'em off about there, an' sew up the ends so they won't ravel out!

CAROLINE (*The idea beginning to dawn on her*): Why, they're for the Army! (*Takes trousers and hugs them to her, legs hanging down.*)

WILFRED: Sh! Don't speak so loud, for heaven's sake! (*He glances back, as if afraid of being overheard.*) I've got a jacket here too! Nearly a fit—came from the hospital—Johnny Sheldon wore it—he won't want it any more, you know—an' he was just about my size!

CAROLINE (*In a low voice*): No—he won't want it any more.

WILFRED (*After a slight pause*): Well! What is it? I thought you said you wanted to help!

CAROLINE (*Quickly*): I do! I do!

FROM **Arms and the Man**

By GEORGE BERNARD SHAW

Neither pure farce nor strict comedy of manners, *Arms and the Man*—as, indeed, all plays by Shaw—is a law unto itself. There are several entertaining two-person scenes in the play. The one given here is for two character actors; the long scene in Act I between Raina and the Man is an excellent choice for an ingenue and a young leading man.

This scene, from Act II, takes place in the garden of Major Petkoff's house. Petkoff has just returned from the wars, and is greeted by his wife.

CATHERINE: My dear Paul: what a surprise for us! (*She stoops over the back of his chair to kiss him.*) Have they brought you fresh coffee?

PETKOFF: Yes: Louka's been looking after me. The war's over. The treaty was signed three days ago at Bucharest; and the decree for our army to demobilize was issued yesterday.

CATHERINE (*Springing erect, with flashing eyes*): Paul: have you let the Austrians force you to make peace?

PETKOFF (*Submissively*): My dear: they didnt consult me. What could *I* do? (*She sits down and turns away from him.*) But of course we saw to it that the treaty was an honorable one. It declares peace—

CATHERINE (*Outraged*): Peace!

PETKOFF (*Appeasing her*): —but not friendly relations: remember that. They wanted to put that in; but I insisted on its being struck out. What more could I do?

CATHERINE: You could have annexed Serbia and made Prince Alexander Emperor of the Balkans. Thats what I would have done.

PETKOFF: I dont doubt it in the least, my dear. But I should have had to subdue the whole Austrian Empire first; and that would have kept me too long away from you. I missed you greatly.

CATHERINE (*Relenting*): Ah! (*She stretches her hand affectionately across the table to squeeze his.*)

PETKOFF: And how have you been, my dear?

CATHERINE: Oh, my usual sore throats: thats all.

PETKOFF (*With conviction*): That comes from washing your neck every day. Ive often told you so.

CATHERINE: Nonsense, Paul!

PETKOFF (*Over his coffee and cigaret*): I dont believe in going too far with these modern customs. All this washing cant be good for the health: it's not natural. There was an Englishman at Philippopolis who used to wet himself all over with cold water every morning when he got up. Disgusting! It all comes from the English: their climate makes them so dirty that they have to be perpetually washing themselves. Look at my father! he never had a bath in his life; and he lived to be ninety-eight, the healthiest man in Bulgaria. I dont mind a good wash once a week to keep up my position; but once a day is carrying the thing to a ridiculous extreme.

CATHERINE: You are a barbarian at heart still, Paul. I hope you behaved yourself before all those Russian officers.

PETKOFF: I did my best. I took care to let them know that we have a library.

CATHERINE: Ah, but you didnt tell them that we have an electric bell in it? I have had one put up.

PETKOFF: Whats an electric bell?

CATHERINE: You touch a button; something tinkles in the kitchen; and then Nicola comes up.

PETKOFF: Why not shout for him?

CATHERINE: Civilized people never shout for their servants. Ive learnt that while you were away.

PETKOFF: Well, I'll tell you something Ive learnt too. Civilized people dont hang out their washing to dry where visitors can see it; so youd better have all that (*indicating the clothes on the bushes*) put somewhere else.

CATHERINE: Oh, thats absurd, Paul: I dont believe really refined people notice such things.

FROM **Medea**

By EURIPIDES,
translated *By* GILBERT MURRAY

The heroic grandeur and stark passion of the Greek tragedies is too often used by inadequate actors as a pretext for posturing, ranting, and all manner of melodramatic emotionalizing. One can be great without being grand; one can be motivated by passion without becoming overwhelmed by it.

This scene of confrontation between Creon, King of Corinth, and Medea, mother of his grandsons, can be subtle, terrifying, and profound without the actors having recourse to theatricalism. It is not easy to achieve the desired effect; but art never is.

CREON: Thou woman sullen-eyed and hot with hate
Against thy lord, Medea, I here command
That thou and thy two children from this land
Go forth to banishment. Make no delay;
Seeing ourselves, the King, are come this day
To see our charge fulfilled; nor shall again
Look homeward ere we have led thy children twain
And thee beyond our realm's last boundary.

MEDEA: Lost! Lost!
Mine haters at the helm with sail flung free
Pursuing; and for us no beach nor shore
In the endless waters! ... Yet, though stricken sore,
I still will ask thee, for what crime, what thing
Unlawful, wilt thou cast me out, O King?

CREON: What crime? I fear thee, woman—little need
To cloak my reasons—lest thou work some deed
Of darkness on my child. And in that fear
Reasons enough have part. Thou comest here
A wise-woman confessed, and full of lore
In unknown ways of evil. Thou art sore
In heart, being parted from thy lover's arms.
And more, thou hast made menace ... so the alarms
But now have reached mine ear ... on bride and
    groom,
And him who gave the bride, to work thy doom
Of vengeance. Which, ere yet it be too late,
I sweep aside. I choose to earn thine hate
Of set will now, not palter with the mood
Of mercy, and hereafter weep in blood.

MEDEA: 'T is not the first nor second time, O King,
That fame hath hurt me, and come nigh to bring
My ruin. ... How can any man, whose eyes
Are wholesome, seek to rear his children wise
Beyond men's wont? Much helplessness in arts
Of common life, and in their townsmen's hearts
Envy deep-set ... so much their learning brings!
Come unto fools with knowledge of new things,
They deem it vanity, not knowledge. Aye,
And men that erst for wisdom were held high,
Feel thee a thorn to fret them, privily
Held higher than they. So hath it been with me.

A wise-woman I am; and for that sin
To divers ill names men would pen me in;
A seed of strife; an eastern dreamer; one
Of brand not theirs; one hard to play upon. ....
Ah, I am not so wondrous wise! And now,
To thee, I am terrible! What fearest thou?
What dire deed? Do I tread so proud a path—
Fear me not thou! —that I should brave the wrath
Of princes? Thou: what hast thou ever done
To wrong me? Granted thine own child to one
Whom thy soul chose. —Ah, *him* out of my heart
I hate; but thou, meseems, hast done thy part
Not ill. And for thine houses' happiness
I hold no grudge. Go: marry, and God bless
Your issues. Only suffer me to rest
Somewhere within this land. Though sore oppressed,
I will be still, knowing mine own defeat.

CREON: Thy words be gentle: but I fear me yet
Lest even now there creep some wickedness
Deep hid within thee. And for that the less
I trust thee now than ere these words began.
A woman quick of wrath, aye, or a man,
Is easier watching than the cold and still.
Up, straight, and find thy road! Mock not my will
With words. This doom is passed beyond recall;
Nor all thy crafts shall help thee, being withal
My manifest foe, to linger at my side.

MEDEA (*Suddenly throwing herself down and cling-
    ing to* CREON):
Oh, by thy knees! By that new-wedded bride ...

CREON: 'T is waste of words. Thou shalt not weaken
    me.

MEDEA: Wilt hunt me? Spurn me when I kneel to thee?

CREON: 'T is mine own house that kneels to me, not thou.

MEDEA: Home, my lost home, how I desire thee now!

CREON: And I mine, and my child, beyond all things.

MEDEA: O Loves of man, what curse is on your wings!

CREON: Blessing or curse, 't is as their chances flow.

MEDEA: Remember, Zeus, the cause of all this woe!

CREON: Oh, rid me of my pains! Up, get thee gone!

MEDEA: What would I with thy pains? I have my own.

CREON: Up: or, 'fore God, my soldiers here shall fling ...

MEDEA: Not that! Not that! ... I do but pray, O King ...

CREON: Thou wilt not? I must face the harsher task?

MEDEA: I accept mine exile. 'T is not that I ask.

CREON: Why then so wild? Why clinging to mine
　　hand?

MEDEA (*Rising*): For one day only leave me in thy
　　land
At peace, to find some counsel, ere the strain
Of exile fall, some comfort for these twain,
Mine innocents; since others take no thought,
It seems, to save the babes that they begot.
Ah! Thou wilt pity them! Thou also art
A father: thou hast somewhere still a heart
That feels. . . . I reck not of myself: 't is they
That break me, fallen upon so dire a day.

CREON: Mine is no tyrant's mood. Aye, many a time
Ere this my tenderness hath marred the chime
Of wisest counsels. And I know that now
I do mere folly. But so be it! Thou
Shalt have this grace . . . But this I warn thee clear,
If once the morrow's sunlight find thee here
Within my borders, thee or child of thine,
Thou diest! . . . Of this judgment not a line
Shall waver nor abate. So linger on,
If thou needs must, till the next risen sun;
No further. . . . In one day there scarce can be
Those perils wrought whose dread yet haunteth me.

FROM **The Road
to Rome**

By ROBERT SHERWOOD

When a dramatist chooses as his subject a
character or an episode from the historical
past, it is usually because he wishes to point
a lesson to his audience of the contemporary
present. Such is certainly the case in *The
Road to Rome*. Sherwood uses Hannibal at
the gates of Rome to point a pacifist moral;
and the fact that the play is a light comedy
does not vitiate the importance of the
author's message.

The dual perspective of such a play, however, presents a unique problem to the
actors. Their style must be neither too contemporary nor too historic. One could not
successfully play Hannibal and Amytis as
though they were characters out of Terence; but they could not be played as mid-
twentieth-century characters either. Where
to draw the line?

For those actors who enjoy the scene below, there is an equally delightful scene
between the same characters in Act II. (The
scene here comes from Act III.)

HANNIBAL: Did you hear my conversation with your husband?

AMYTIS: Yes—I heard it all.

HANNIBAL: I delayed my decision—because I wanted to give you your choice. Last night I should have put you to death. I shouldn't have listened to a word of protest or persuasion. But I did listen—and you didn't die.... This morning, it is different.... I can't destroy Rome until I know what your choice is to be.... I will spare your husband's life. You can go back to him, and I'll see that you both are allowed to escape—to go wherever you please...that's one part of your choice, Amytis.

AMYTIS: And the other part?

HANNIBAL: To go with me. To forget Rome—to forget Carthage—to be with me forever...

AMYTIS: And if I agree to that part of it, will Rome be spared?

HANNIBAL (*Emphatically*): No! Whatever your choice, Rome must be destroyed.

AMYTIS: Then I choose to go back to my husband.... Go ahead with your great work, Hannibal. Burn Rome to the ground; obliterate it. Keep your army here forever, to make sure Rome stays destroyed. Instruct your men to crush any blade of grass, any flower that dares to thrust its head above the ashes of the dead city. Prolong your victory. Glory in it till your dying day.... But don't ever look to me, or to my memory, for sympathy or applause.

HANNIBAL (*Angrily*): I think I understand you at last. You came here to save Rome. If you fail in that, you're prepared to die. For all your talk, you care nothing for me.

AMYTIS: You mustn't believe that, Hannibal.
(*There is a shrill bugle call.*)

HANNIBAL: You thought you could save Rome from the destiny that is ready to overwhelm it! You have tried to build walls of words as a defense against my army.

AMYTIS: I'm not trying to save Rome, Hannibal. I'm trying to save you.

HANNIBAL: Why do you imagine that I'm worth saving?

AMYTIS: Because I want to have you—always—as my possession. Let Rome and Carthage remember you as a great general. I want to remember you as a conqueror who could realize the glory of submission.

HANNIBAL (*Challenging*): And does Rome realize the glory of submission?

AMYTIS: No, and for that very reason Rome will destroy itself. Success is like a strong wine, Hannibal; give a man enough of it, and he'll drink himself to death. Rome will do that, too, if you leave it alone.

HANNIBAL: So I'm to leave Rome—and to leave you. Is that your choice?

AMYTIS: Yes, Hannibal—to leave me with something beautiful—something that is worth remembering. I don't want you to spoil that.

HANNIBAL: And what shall I have to remember? That I marched three thousand miles—and failed.

AMYTIS: Ah, but that's just the point, Hannibal. You haven't failed.

HANNIBAL: I came to conquer Rome. Anything short of that is failure.

AMYTIS: Are you sure of that? Are you sure that you didn't come all this way to find your own soul?

HANNIBAL: My own soul doesn't matter, Amytis. I myself amount to nothing. All of us amount to nothing. . . . We stand aside and watch ourselves parade by! We're proud of the brave manner in which we step forward, and of the nobility of our bearing, and the sparkle of divine fire that is in our eyes—and actually we have no more idea of where we're going, no more choice in the matter, than so many drops of water in a flowing river.

AMYTIS: Yes, and at the end of that river is an endless sea of things that are passed. It is called history. When you reach that sea, other drops of water may murmur respectfully, "Here comes Hannibal, the conqueror of Rome." But you won't care.

You'll only be thankful for the interludes that you have known—the moments when you drifted from the main current and found peace and contentment in the deep, quiet pools.

(*They are standing close together, facing each other. With sudden, fierce strength,* HANNIBAL *takes her in his arms.*)

HANNIBAL: I'll turn away from Rome now, Amytis, if you'll come with me.... Rome can live, Amytis. You can save it...

AMYTIS: I don't want it to be that way...

HANNIBAL: I'll bury my sword before the gates of Rome. I'll hand over my command to Hasdrubal. I'll do the one thing I thought was impossible: I'll quit when I'm winning. But I can't do this alone...I can't...

AMYTIS: No, Hannibal. I don't want it to be that way. I don't want Rome to be saved because I made this choice.... I want you to do it—to make the decision—to prove that you are stronger than your own victorious army...

HANNIBAL: If I recognize your truths, I'll have to believe that all my life has been wasted—that all those men who have fallen along the road to Rome have died for nothing. Do you want me to believe that?

AMYTIS: I do! I do! I want you to believe that every sacrifice made in the name of war is wasted. When you believe that, you'll be a great man. (*Gently, she strokes his hair.*) I want you to be a great man.

Lady Windermere's Fan

By OSCAR WILDE

Oscar Wilde's reputation as a playwright rests so securely on the brillance of his epigrammatic dialogue that it is easy to forget how skilled a craftsman he was when it came to dramaturgy. In *Lady Windermere's Fan*, the central issue is hopelessly outdated, and so are the technical devices by which Wilde maneuvered his plot. Yet Wilde's grasp of dramatic character was so strong, his pacing of dialogue so accurate, that scenes like the following (their over-formal language notwithstanding) retain enormous theatrical vitality to this day.

The scene is the morning room in Lord Windermere's house. Windermere is disconcerted by the arrival of the notorious Mrs. Erlynne, the "woman with a past" whom he knows to be his wife's mother. The scene occurs in the middle of Act IV.

MRS. ERLYNNE: You seem rather out of temper this morning, Windermere. Why should you be? Margaret and I get on charmingly together.

WINDERMERE: I can't bear to see you with her. Besides, you have not told me the truth, Mrs. Erlynne.

MRS. ERLYNNE: I have not told *her* the truth, you mean.

WINDERMERE: I sometimes wish you had. I should have been spared then the misery, the anxiety, the annoyance of the last six months. But rather than my wife should know—that the mother whom she was taught to consider as dead, the mother whom she has mourned as dead, is living—a divorced woman going under an assumed name, a bad woman preying upon life, as I know you now to be—rather than that, I was ready to supply you with money to pay bill after bill, extravagance after extravagance, to risk what occurred yesterday, the first quarrel I have ever had with my wife. You don't understand what that means to me. How could you? But I tell you that the only bitter words that ever came from those sweet lips of hers were on your account, and I hate to see you next to her. You sully the innocence that is in her. And then I used to think that with all your faults you were frank and honest. You are not.

MRS. ERLYNNE: Why do you say that?

WINDERMERE: You made me get you an invitation to my wife's ball.

MRS. ERLYNNE: For my daughter's ball—yes.

WINDERMERE: You came, and within an hour of your leaving the house, you are found in a man's rooms—you are disgraced before everyone. (*Goes up center.*)

MRS. ERLYNNE: Yes.

WINDERMERE (*Turning round on her*): Therefore I have a right to look upon you as what you are—a worthless, vicious woman. I have the right to tell you never to enter this house, never to attempt to come near my wife—

MRS. ERLYNNE (*Coldly*): My daughter, you mean.

WINDERMERE: You have no right to claim her as your daughter. You left her, abandoned her, when she was but a child in the cradle, abandoned her for your lover, who abandoned you in turn.

MRS. ERLYNNE (*Rising*): Do you count that to his credit, Lord Windermere—or to mine?

WINDERMERE: To his, now that I know you.

MRS. ERLYNNE: Take care—you had better be careful.

WINDERMERE: Oh, I am not going to mince words for you. I know you thoroughly.

MRS. ERLYNNE (*Looking steadily at him*): I question that.

WINDERMERE: I *do* know you. For twenty years of your life you lived without your child, without a thought of your child. One day you read in the papers that she had married a rich man. You saw your hideous chance. You knew that to spare her the ignominy of learning that a woman like you was her mother, I would endure anything. You began your blackmailing.

MRS. ERLYNNE (*Shrugging her shoulders*): Don't use ugly words, Windermere. They are vulgar. I saw my chance, it is true, and took it.

WINDERMERE: Yes, you took it—and spoiled it all last night, by being found out.

MRS. ERLYNNE (*With a strange smile*): You are quite right. I spoiled it all last night.

WINDERMERE: And as for your blunder in taking my wife's fan from her, and then leaving it about in Darlington's rooms, it is unpardonable. I can't bear the sight of it now. I shall never let my wife use it again. The thing is soiled for me. You should have kept it, and not brought it back.

MRS. ERLYNNE: I think I *shall* keep it. (*Goes up.*) It's extremely pretty. (*Takes up fan.*) I shall ask Margaret to give it to me.

WINDERMERE: I hope my wife will give it to you.

MRS. ERLYNNE: Oh, I'm sure she will have no objection.

WINDERMERE: I wish at the same time she would give you a miniature she kisses every night before she prays—it's the miniature of a young, innocent-looking girl with beautiful dark hair.

MRS. ERLYNNE: Ah, yes, I remember. How long ago that seems! (*Goes to sofa and sits down.*) It was done before I was married. Dark hair and an innocent expression were the fashion then, Windermere! (*A pause.*)

WINDERMERE: What do you mean by coming here this morning? What is your object?

MRS. ERLYNNE (*With a note of irony in her voice*): To bid good-bye to my dear daughter, of course. (WINDERMERE *bites his underlip in anger.* MRS. ERLYNNE *looks at him, and her voice and manner become serious. In her accents as she talks there is a note of deep tragedy. For a moment, she reveals herself.*)

MRS. ERLYNNE: Oh, don't imagine I am going to have a pathetic scene with her, weep on her neck and tell her who I am, and all that kind of thing. I have no ambition to play the part of a mother. Only once in my life have I known a mother's feelings. That was last night. They were terrible—they made me suffer—they made me suffer too much. For twenty years, as you say, I have lived childless—I want to live childless still. (*Hiding her feelings with a trivial laugh*): Besides, my dear Windermere, how on earth could I pose as a mother with a grown up daughter?

Margaret is twenty-one, and I have never admitted that I am more than twenty-nine, or thirty at the most. Twenty-nine when there are pink shades, thirty when there are not. So you see what difficulties it would involve. No, as far as I am concerned, let your wife cherish the memory of this dead, stainless mother. Why should I interfere with her illusions? I find it hard enough to keep my own. I lost one illusion last night. I thought I had no heart. I find I have, and a heart doesn't suit me, Windermere. Somehow it doesn't go with modern dress. It makes one look old.

FROM **Venus Observed**

By CHRISTOPHER FRY

The British theater of the mid-twentieth-
century saw the flowering of two major verse
dramatists: T. S. Eliot and Christopher Fry.
Of the two, Fry was perhaps the less profound; his work, however, was the more
theatrically successful. *The Lady's Not for
Burning* enjoyed long runs in both London
and New York, and is frequently seen in
revival.

In Fry's less well-known *Venus Observed*,
the intelligent, middle-aged Duke of Altair
is in search of a second wife. Unexpectedly,
his choice is widened by the appearance of
his estate manager's young and beautiful
daughter, Perpetua Reedbeck. Almost the
whole of Act II, Scene 2, is devoted to the
late-night meeting of this pair in the Ob-
servatory Tower of the Duke's ancestral
home; the extract below comes from the
middle of this scene. Actors may wish also
to use as scenes for study the preceding and
following dialogues between the same characters.

PERPETUA: Why are you so sure
That I must love you? The field is wide,
And everyone's heart is a great eccentric;
Its whole distinction is a madness. Wildly
Away from any mark it goes, making
Anywhere the same gigantic mimicry of sunshine,
No one else knows why. Be sure of nothing.

DUKE: Do you know what night this is?

PERPETUA: All-Hallows' Eve.

DUKE: All-Hallows' Eve. If the earth is ever wise
To magic, this is the night when magic's wisdom
Comes rolling in across our sedate equation.
All the closed hours unlock; the rigorous ground
Grows as soft as the sea, exhaling
The bloom of the dead everywhere. They almost
Live again: as nearly, at least, as we
Can brush on death. And through the night
They trespass agreeably on our time of trespasses,
Molesting the air in a pale, disinterested
Way, until they thankfully notice
The dark is paler, and sigh themselves out again;
Though not before they've planted, as they go,
A seed of chill which grows rapidly
Into a rigid winter where the sun
Can hardly raise himself to make a noon.
But still, that's presently. What's more to our purpose
Is that to-night the gravity of mirrors
Is so potent it can draw the future
Into the glass, and show shadows of husbands
To girls who sit and comb their hair. Suppose
You try it.

PERPETUA: I'm two or three centuries
Too late.

DUKE: We know nothing yet.
There's the mirror. In your bag no doubt
A comb. And while you comb tradition says
You must eat an apple: though God knows why
Any apple should trust itself between your teeth
After this morning's little episode.
However, here's one intrepid to the core.

PERPETUA: How old is this mirror? The glass
Is very loath to let me in.

DUKE: Eight duchesses
Have rested there in passing, before the glass
Began to cloud; and after that came three
Peering housekeepers, a chambermaid
Who, what with frequent tears and the ageing mirror,
Never saw her face; and me, who by
Much early study have overcome the need
To try.

PERPETUA: And I am the eight duchesses
And the three housekeepers and the chambermaid
Combing their hair. I am any girl: Perpetua
Perpetual, making no gesture I can call
My own, engraving theirs one lifetime deeper.
Midnight, the apple, and Perpetua
Combing her hair, as all the time she was.
(The DUKE *quietly crosses the room until his reflec-*
tion falls into the mirror. PERPETUA's *attention is*
caught; she stares into the glass before she turns
suddenly to look at The DUKE.)
It seemed to be your son.

DUKE: Perpetua,
You must play fair.

PERPETUA: You must tell that to the mirror.
The reflection seemed to be Edgar.

DUKE: Then the mirror
Is very penetrating. It has seen
How young, to all intents, I am.

PERPETUA: I suppose so.
You think there's no magic.

DUKE: That's as kind
As anything you've said. I think there *is*
Magic: an old dim-sighted mirror
And a shaded lamp for one genial moment
Raised me out of the falling leaves. A pity
The vision has gone. I'll agree to immortality
If immortality is to be always twenty-five
Seen by a man approaching fifty. The thought
Alone sends me begging to Olympus.
And you, being twenty-five, and looked upon
By me, together we make one golden flesh
For which both worlds, this and the next, will try
To outbid each other, and while the bidding mounts
We'll spend our love between them, disregarding
Both, until—

PERPETUA: Until, next year,
I am twenty-six.

DUKE: Which is twenty-five and one more.
I am the one.

PERPETUA: It remains for me to love you.

DUKE: It has always been understood to be so easy.
Why ever should you not? Am I, before
God, too old? Consider the rocks
Of Arizona, and then consider me.
How recently the world has had the pleasure
Of pleasing, the opportunity of knowing me.
Age, after all, is only the accumulation
Of extensive childhood: what we were,
Never what we are. Don't deliver me
Up to my gray hairs.

PERPETUA: Them I could certainly
Love. No, it's rather that I wonder
Whether you're not almost too young to be lived
    with.

DUKE: When we're married I shall age beside you;
    forgive me
Loitering now till you draw level.

PERPETUA: When we're married?

DUKE: Are we to be formal?
Should I have asked you first?

PERPETUA: Not if you have
Some other way of knowing the answer. Have you?

DUKE: Perhaps I may pass that question back.
    Have I?

FROM **The Magnificent Yankee**

By EMMET LAVERY

When thinking of vital theater, one seldom thinks of biographical drama. And yet such plays—from *Henry VI* to *Hadrian VII*—have held audiences enthralled for centuries (and have given many actors their meatiest roles). *The Magnificent Yankee*, the dramatized story of Mr. Justice Holmes, certainly proved its popularity, both as a play and as a film.

In addition to this scene from Act I, Scene 2, between Holmes and his wife, Fanny, there is an excellent scene for student actors in the Holmes-Secretary scene near the end of Act III. (It should be noted that the secretary is a young man.) The action passes in the library of Holmes's gracious Washington residence, March, 1904.

HOLMES: Now, you little she-devil, what do you mean going around telling people that you are the *second* Mrs. Holmes?

FANNY: Well, how do I know you don't wish there *had* been a second Mrs. Holmes?

HOLMES: Now, Fanny—

FANNY: Besides, I didn't tell Mr. Palmer anything. He just drew his own conclusions. Being so overcome at *not* finding the great man's wife with one foot in the grave, he naturally assumed—

HOLMES: I see. And what are the people back in Boston going to think of all this?

FANNY: Do you care what the people in Boston think? Back there you were merely the good-looking son of the famous Autocrat of the Breakfast Table. To them you were just some sort of literary ornament on the bench, more brilliant than sound. To them—

HOLMES: Hold on. Are you for Boston or against it?

FANNY: Oh, I'm not particular. Pick any side you want and I'll take the opposite.

HOLMES: Woman, what's got into you today? Isn't that another new dress?

FANNY: Yes, milord. Do you like it?

HOLMES: Hmm. Devilish pretty. But not half so pretty as the woman wearing it.

FANNY: Oh, thank you, milord.

HOLMES: Or so devilish either!

FANNY: You're a horrid old man and I hope Mr. Roosevelt beats you with the biggest stick he has.

Oh, I almost forgot. This came for you in the afternoon mail. It was marked personal—so I thought you *might* like to open it yourself. (FANNY *hands him the letter, goes to the door, but stops and watches him as he reads.*) Well, Wendell—who is she? Is she pretty?

HOLMES (*Softly*): Yes. She's pretty—very pretty. Eh? What's that? Oh now, don't misunderstand me. It's nothing—nothing at all. For just a moment I was back at Antietam ... on the road to Hagerstown with a bullet in my neck ... and no one to care for me until the Kennedys took me in ... and a girl named Ellen Jones nursed me back to health ... I never saw her again but she's in town now and ...

FANNY (*Briskly*): Well, let's have her out to dinner by all means.

HOLMES (*Embarrassed*): Yes, that would be very nice but ... she wants to know if I'll have dinner with her at the Shoreham some night.

FANNY: The Shoreham?

HOLMES: That's where she's stopping. Of course it's all a little silly. I don't want to go at all but—

FANNY: Don't be absurd, Wendell. Of course you want to go!

HOLMES: You don't think I should though—do you?

FANNY: My dear, what possible difference could it make to me? It's only that—

HOLMES: Only what?

FANNY: Some people do change, you know...in forty-two years...even if you don't.

HOLMES (*Spontaneously*): Oh, not Ellen Jones. She was the prettiest thing that ever came out of Philadelphia. She— I mean—well, it can't be forty-two years, Fanny. It can't be. Why, it was only yesterday. I can still hear the pound of cannon in the hills...I can still smell the powder burning. I can—

FANNY: Can you still smell the perfume she used? Or has she changed the brand by now, perhaps?

HOLMES: Fanny—you're not jealous—not at this late date?

FANNY: What do you mean by "this late date"? Was there a time when it would have been quite in order for me to be jealous of Miss Jones?

HOLMES: Now, Fanny—

FANNY: I always knew that half the girls in Boston had lost their hearts to you...but I had never given a thought to Philadelphia.

HOLMES: Woman, I'll have you know that in a democracy a man can still look at a pretty woman without violating either his marriage vows on the one hand or the Constitution of the United States on the other.

FANNY: Don't you talk about the Constitution to

me, Mr. Holmes. Save that for Mr. Roosevelt. If you want to spend an evening mooning over the dear old days with an elderly hussy from Philadelphia—

HOLMES: She's not a hussy.

FANNY: —why, you go right ahead. I have no objections. Only don't bring the Constitution into it. Take her some nice flowers—buy her a good wine and a wonderful dinner. But leave the Constitution home. You won't need it!

Copies of this play, individual paper covered acting editions, are available from Samuel French, Inc., 25 West 45th Street, New York, New York or 7623 Sunset Boulevard, Hollywood, California, or in Canada Samuel French, (Canada) Ltd., 26 Grenville Street, Toronto, Canada.

FROM **The Cage**

By MARIO FRATTI,
translated *By* MARGUERITA CARRA and
LOUISE WARNER

Although there is always the danger of over-simplification when one uses labels and catch phrases by which to pigeon-hole plays, the terms "theater of the absurd" and "black comedy" do help to understand much of what is being written for the theater today. Playwrights are more and more attracted by the odd, the freakish, the bizarre in their search for new symbols.

The central character of Mario Fratti's play, Cristiano, has freely chosen to live in a cage in the main room of his family's flat. His behavior is a source of embarrassment, inconvenience, and frustration to them, but he refuses to leave his cell. As a result, family life must proceed almost as though he were not there as a perpetual spectator.

In this scene, Cristiano, inside his cage, engages in conversation with his sister-in-law, Chiara. There is another good scene for the same two characters earlier in the act (Act II), just after Pietro's exit.

CHIARA (*Sitting on the bed, taking her housecoat off*): You behaved badly.

CRISTIANO: What about you? (CHIARA *looks at him questioningly, surprised by his tone and attitude.*) You looked like the "Sinner in an Old Portrait"... (*Morbidly*): half naked, washing your legs... (*He contemplates her breasts.*)

CHIARA: I had my housecoat on.

CRISTIANO: Wide open...

CHIARA: As usual... After all, he had his back to me.

CRISTIANO: You let him kiss you.

CHIARA (*Teasingly*): Cristiano, it was a friendly kiss, nothing more. You're the one who's making something out of it. (*Coquettishly*): More friendly than that kiss you gave me before... on my hand... (*She looks straight into his eyes,* CRISTIANO *feels uncomfortable.*) He's an impulsive young man, sincere...

CRISTIANO (*In desperation*): No, no, it's not true! This is your mistake. To believe in the sincerity of others.

CHIARA (*Calmly*): He seems sincere to me. What makes you think otherwise?

CRISTIANO (*Emphatically*): No one is sincere in this world! You're not when you "accept" your husband (*pointing to the bed*). He's not (*pointing to the door from which* SERGIO *left*) when he preaches. Why do you think we have missionaries? Because they want to be leaders of a flock, no matter how small it may be ... They pretend to love the weak, the ignorant. Why? Because they want to lead a fraction of humanity. No one is sincere in this world.

CHIARA (*Slowly*): He offered you a chance to become a "leader," in their library.

CRISTIANO: I don't care.

CHIARA: He ran the risk of being ousted by you. You're cultured, you've read more than he. He might lose his "leadership" by letting you in.

CRISTIANO: He knew perfectly well that I wouldn't accept.

CHIARA: You accuse him of bad faith, then.

CRISTIANO: Like everyone else.

CHIARA: Even your mother?

CRISTIANO: Yes ... when she pretends to feel sorry for me. She has her outbursts which she checks with difficulty. I sense it ... even though she's learned to control herself.

CHIARA (*Slowly studying him*): One question. According to you, can one lie out of pity, love?

CRISTIANO: No.

CHIARA: It takes courage to be sincere. Do you have it?

CRISTIANO: Yes.

CHIARA: With whom?

CRISTIANO: With everyone.

CHIARA: With us perhaps. The few people you know because you feel protected by those bars.

CRISTIANO: With everyone.

CHIARA: How commendable! You're the only one, then, who is sincere? (CRISTIANO *doesn't answer.*) Everyone else in this house lies?

CRISTIANO: Everyone, even your husband who despises you and then... (*Points to bed.*)

CHIARA (*Ignoring the allusion*): Even your sister?

CRISTIANO: Even my sister. You've seen her—she's more "feminine" when he's here! She deceives him with her play acting, by pretending she's in love.

CHIARA: Isn't she?

CRISTIANO (*Hesitantly*): I don't know...

CHIARA: How can *you* judge love? You don't know what it is. (*Almost to herself, with passion*): It's a fever that consumes you, a desire to touch the one you love, to lose yourself in him, to belong to him, to be beautiful. Your sister wants to appear better in Sergio's eyes. Your sister is in love.

CRISTIANO: She just wants to get out of this house. She wants a change.

CHIARA: Even that is love. To escape from the present, which is "putrid," as you describe it, for a better life, in the future . . .

CRISTIANO: Even the "future" is putrid.

CHIARA: In your books.

CRISTIANO: These books confirm what I've seen out there.

CHIARA: How many years were you "out there," among men?

CRISTIANO: Long enough for me to know them. I'm afraid of them. I'm afraid of myself . . . because . . . (*Excitedly*): I could kill, yes . . . I would kill those who lie, flatter, ridicule.

CHIARA (*Again to herself, fascinated by the idea*): "To kill" . . .

CRISTIANO (*Tormenting himself*): Yes. I feel I have the strength, the will. Why do you think I locked myself behind these bars? Because I even hate all of you . . . (*Wringing his hands*): I could even kill all of you. To control oneself is a superhuman effort. These bars help me. (*With bowed head he withdraws into himself.*)

FROM Scuba Duba

By BRUCE JAY FRIEDMAN

A triumphant comedy hit of the 1967–68 Off-Broadway season, *Scuba Duba* concerns a white, middle-class, Jewish advertising copywriter named Harold Wonder, spending the summer in France with his family. His wife, Jean, has just run off with another man (a Negro scuba diver of recent acquaintance, thinks Harold). Act I details the events of the night following Jean's departure. (There are several long, funny dialogues for Harold and the girl next door, Miss Janus, which would make excellent scenes for study.) In this scene, early in Act II, Jean returns to the apartment for the first time.

JEAN: Harold... How are you?...

HAROLD: What do I know?...

JEAN: How are the kids?

HAROLD: They're fine, under the circumstances. You all right?

JEAN: Pretty good. My arm hurts though.

HAROLD: What happened?

JEAN: I think I got gas in it.

HAROLD: What do you mean gas? You can't have gas in your arm.

JEAN: No, that's what it is. I'm sure of it. Somehow it curled around through here and got right into my arm. It'll be all right.

HAROLD: It's not gas. Remember that party? What was it, Friends of the Middle East? You were positive you were having a heart attack. *That* was gas.

JEAN: That was a small heart attack, Harold. I just accepted it and when it was over I was grateful and that was the end of it.

HAROLD: Everything else all right?

JEAN: My neck is a little tensed up. I'm just going to have to live with that. (*She starts to dust.*) You okay?

HAROLD: Jeannie, don't dust now, will you?

JEAN: Well, what am I supposed to do, leave it there, just let it accumulate? Breathe it all in? Foreign dust. How do we know what's in it?

HAROLD: There's nothing in it. It's just a little

French dust. No dusting now, okay? Will you do me
that favor. I'm trying to get a little sore. There's something that happens to your shoulders—when you
dust—and I don't want to get involved in that now.
They get frail or something. I probably never told
you, but I can't stand to see you dust. It's like I took
this young, fragrant, hopeful, beautiful young girl and
turned her into an old cleaning lady.

JEAN: Women like to dust, silly. It doesn't hurt
them.

HAROLD: Well it hurts the hell out of me. I can't
stand it. (*She stops dusting.*)

JEAN: How about you? In your bathrobe. I can
stand that? And making that face at me...

HAROLD: Which one's that?

JEAN: You know which one. There's only one. You
made it at Gloria Novak's wedding reception, the
first time I ever saw you. At the salad table. I looked
up from my salad and I see this big guy making a
face at me.

HAROLD: I don't know what you're talking about.

JEAN: Not much. That little boy face. Whenever you
want something. Look at you. You can't even switch
off to another one, even right now. You did it to me
then and you're doing it right now.

HAROLD: What I'm doing right this second, right
now?

JEAN: That's right.

HAROLD: I never made this face before in my life.

JEAN: Right. I just came in here . . . I was going to get a few things . . . (*Starts for bedroom.*)

HAROLD (*Intercepting her*): No things, no things. That's one line I never want to hear. (*In British accent*): "Dudley, I've come for my things." Anybody gets their things, that's the end of their things. In this house you get your *stuff*, hear? And you don't get that either. . . . This is some mess.

JEAN: I know.

HAROLD: I think this is the worst we ever had.

JEAN: I don't know, Harold. I think when I was pregnant and we couldn't get any heat in the apartment and you had to organize a warmth committee in the building at four in the morning. I think that was worse.

HAROLD: No, I think this is worse. I had a lot of people on my side in that one. I had the whole building cheering me on. I'm all alone on this one.

JEAN: What kind of alone? You think I'm loving this? That I'm loving every second of it . . .

HAROLD: You're loving it more than I am. Anybody'd be loving it more than I am. There's not one person I can think of who wouldn't be loving this more than I am. . . . You think we'll get out of it?

JEAN: I don't know, Harold. At this point I'd settle for just getting through the morning.

HAROLD (*On his knees, cracking*): Ah come on, Pidge, will you just quit it right now. Will you get the hell back home. Will you just stay here. What do you want to do, ship me off to Happydale? I'm down here on the floor. I'm not a guy who does that.

JEAN (*Comforting*): I know, Harold, I know.

HAROLD (*Recovering slightly*): Look, there's just one thing I have to find out. This is important. Did you get into things like Pidge? Does he know I call you Pidge?

JEAN: That's what you consider important? That's what this is all about to you? Pidge?

HAROLD: No, seriously, I just have to know that one thing and then I'll never bother you again.

JEAN: I may have said something...

HAROLD (*Leaping up in triumph*): You told him Pidge. That's probably the first thing you blurted out. I was just on the floor where I've never been in my life—and you had to tell him Pidge. I was just hoping you'd keep one thing separate, one little private area so that maybe we could start battling our way back, inch by inch, to being a little bit together again. What you did is just fork it right over ...

JEAN: I don't remember if I told him...

HAROLD (*Not hearing her*): All right, number one, cancel what I just did on the floor. And number two, drag in that chocolate shithead. I've been waiting for this all night.

JEAN: Harold, could you try to be a little dignified. I can get that style from my father. I don't need it from you. I grew up with that. You know, for a second I really felt a little something—the first time in years—and then you have just heaved it right out of the window.

FROM Goat Song

By FRANZ WERFEL

Franz Werfel, best known perhaps for his novel *The Forty Days of Musa Dagh*, contributed at least one major play to the body of world dramatic literature: *Goat Song*, a symbolic, pageant-like depiction of the spread of man's brutality. Set in the eighteenth century in a Slavic countryside beyond the Danube, the play has an earthy folk quality that brings its language close to poetry.

Mirko and Stanja have been betrothed. In this scene from Act I, Scene 5, the couple enters the farmhouse of Mirko's father, after the lad has taken his bride-to-be, Stanja, on a tour of his family's property.

MIRKO: Your parents are gone now. Are you sad?

STANJA: No, I am not sad.

MIRKO: Then you don't love your parents?

STANJA: I love them.

MIRKO: Then you must be sad. Doesn't it hurt you when something is over? The axle creaks, the horses draw up, the whip.... And then, something is ended.

STANJA: I never ache for what is past.

MIRKO: Oh, I often do. I can lie in the meadow hour after hour longing for the games I played there on the grass.

STANJA: That is because you are a man. (*Short pause.*)

MIRKO: Do the house and the farm please you?

STANJA: Why shouldn't they? House, rooms, chimneys, stables, pigsties, and hencoops and dovecotes, same as everywhere.

MIRKO: And do I please you?

STANJA: Why shouldn't you please me?

MIRKO: Do you know, Stanja, I would have liked it better if you had cried before, when they left you.... (*Suddenly turns on her.*) You! What if you've loved someone before! Tell me! Have you loved someone else?

STANJA (*Hesitatingly*): No.

MIRKO (*Slowly, his eyes closed*): I think, when we're married, I will beat you.

STANJA: That's what all husbands do.

MIRKO: Did you tell me the truth?

STANJA: No.

MIRKO: Ah! You did love another before me, before me ...

STANJA: Did I love him? Just once, I dreamed of him in the night. He'd been our guest for an hour. He wore a scholar's cap on his head and a laced coat. He was a student.

MIRKO (*Presses her hand*): Did he speak to you? Did you see him again? Or dream of him?

STANJA: Never again.

MIRKO (*Lets her hand fall, brusquely*): A student? Ho! You want to show me you're a smart one.

STANJA (*Flashing*): That takes no showing.

MIRKO: Damn!

STANJA: You led me through the rooms and closets up to the attic. We looked at all the stalls, the cattle, the dairies, the storehouse, the threshing floors, wine presses, everything. But I have eyes ...

MIRKO (*Excited, tries to embrace her*): Blue eyes, sharp, bad, sweet. ...

STANJA (*Thrusts him from her*): But mighty quick you slipped by that little house of stone, and by that rusty iron door. You wouldn't look, and pushed me away. (*Triumphant*): What does the smoking chimney of that big kennel mean? You light no fire for animals. That rising smoke is human.... I have eyes!

MIRKO (*Stroking his forehead in helpless bewilderment*): I do not know, Stanja. Believe me, I do not know. Ever since I was a little child that was the forbidden place that we hurried by in fear, with downcast eyes. I dared not ask my mother or my father. I love my—father—not as you love yours. So I kept still and let my father bear the secret. I got used to it as a child and never gave it thought. But now! For twenty years, day after day, I have passed it—and always with my foreboding heart, yet never thinking of it. And now, all of a sudden, after so many years, I'm forced to think.... Yes, true enough! A fire's there each spring and winter. (*Seized by an obscure horror*): Stanja! I will not ask my father. I'll never ask.

STANJA: Now do you see who is the smart one? For twenty years you never thought or asked. But a woman comes to the house and asks you the first hour.

part 2

Scenes for Two Men

FROM **Edward, My Son**

By ROBERT MORLEY and
NOEL LANGLEY

Although neither an important play nor a distinguished one, *Edward, My Son* was both successful and popular. It is therefore worthy of study. Among its qualities—qualities which it shares with many another successful play in the so-called "commercial" theater—are clearly defined characters with strong motivation, tight dramatic construction, unpretentious dialogue, and a certain verve that might best be called theatricality.

In this scene from Act II, Scene 1, the eminently successful and ambitous business-man Arnold Holt grants an interview to Harry Soames, who has recently been released from jail (or "gaol" as the British spelling has it). The men are the same age, but in quite different life circumstances.

Act I, Scene 3, comprises a dialogue for the same characters, before Soames's imprisonment; and there is another good scene for two men in Act I, Scene 4, between Holt and a character called Hanray.

ARNOLD: My dear fellow... Come in. Good to see you again.

SOAMES: Is it?

ARNOLD: Certainly it is... you're looking fine. (*To his* SECRETARY *at the door*): Miss Perry, I don't want to be disturbed for about five minutes. Sit down, Harry.

SOAMES: Thanks... I hear you've got Burton working for you now?

ARNOLD: Yes. I thought I'd better look after him for you, Harry, but if you want him back, you've only got to say so.

SOAMES: Thanks. Is he *your* confidential secretary these days?

ARNOLD: No. I've still got Miss Perry.

SOAMES: I think you're wise at that. Burton sold me out. The dirty little rat.

ARNOLD: Now listen, Harry, you've got to get hold of yourself. Talking like that won't get you anywhere... besides, it's not true.

SOAMES: How the hell do you know?

ARNOLD: I know he's a decent fellow.

SOAMES: He sold me out to someone and they

tipped off the police... another twenty-four hours would have seen me right. I'd like to find out who paid him to do it, that's all.

ARNOLD: Why should anyone pay him?

SOAMES: You don't think I have any enemies? Maybe you're right. Perhaps it was one of my friends. Well, I haven't any proof, so let's forget it, shall we?

ARNOLD: I think you'd be wiser to forget it, Harry... all of it.

SOAMES: Maybe.

ARNOLD: How are the family?

SOAMES: I guess they're fine, thanks. Mabel has a job in a tea shop and Arthur is a van boy. Making good money, too, all of two pounds a week.

ARNOLD: I wrote to Mabel, you know, offering her any help I could give... I never got a reply.

SOAMES: She told me. It was good of you. I guess she's got more pride than I have. Fiona, the little one, remember?

ARNOLD: Of course I do.

SOAMES: She got a scholarship to the London University.

ARNOLD: Oh, that was splendid.

SOAMES: She couldn't afford to go, so she's working in a shop now. Gee, I'd like to see them again!

ARNOLD: Well, you will soon.

SOAMES: No, I don't expect to see them for quite a time, Arnold, not till I've got one or two things straightened out. I think I've caused them enough harm to be going on with.

ARNOLD: Now, Harry, you mustn't feel like that. (*The telephone rings.*) Hullo. Yes. Put him through. (*To* SOAMES): Excuse me. Hullo, Edward? Where are you? At the station? Good. What? Oh, nonsense, you'll have a whale of a time. I wish I could have, old man. Well, yes, maybe. What? But you had fifty pounds last week. All of it? Yes, that's all very well, what's your mother going to say? (*He laughs.*) I expect she will. What do you want me to do? That's no use, she'd see the letter. Certainly I'd have to register it. I could do that, I suppose. Do you think there's more than one Post Office? Oh. Well, I suppose we boys have to stick together. But Edward, do try and be a bit more careful. That's all right. Have a good time. Oh, I say, while you're out there you might go and see Schmitt. You remember him? Might be the smart thing to do. Oh, Edward, give my love to your mother. Oh yes, I forgot, so she would. Well, goodbye then. (*He rings off.*) He'll be a wonderful business man . . . He never misses a trick . . . (*He turns to* SOAMES.) What were we talking about?

SOAMES: Our children.

ARNOLD: Yes. Well, look, if there's anything I can do for them, you only have to ask.

SOAMES: Thanks. I'll remember that.

ARNOLD: And now the next question is, what can we do for you? Just a moment— (*Into the dictaphone*): Miss Perry, wire Mr. Edward fifty pounds Poste Restante, St. Moritz. Yes, that's right. No, not for the Hotel. Better make it seventy-five pounds. (*To* SOAMES): Got any plans?

SOAMES: No, not a great many. I don't find it quite so easy to make them as I did. I'm getting old, I suppose.

ARNOLD: Nonsense!

SOAMES: Perhaps just discouraged. Mind you, I'm not kicking against my trial or my sentence, they were fair enough. What gets me is that twice in my life I've been fool enough to try and get away with it, each time I told myself that I wouldn't be the one to get caught. All around me I saw other men taking the chances I took: they got through all right. Why shouldn't I? I know men and so do you, not a hundred yards away from this desk, who are much bigger crooks than I ever was; who break the law over and over again. And they do worse than that; they get around the law and squirm under it and climb above it and what happens to them? Nothing. That's what burns me up. It's so damned unfair—I only wanted what they wanted, not as much as most of 'em. I wanted money for my wife and kids and a decent home and a respectable old age.

ARNOLD: What you need, my boy, is work.

SOAMES: What sort of work would you suggest?

ARNOLD: Well, how about starting a little business somewhere? An antique shop, or a tobacconist; that's one of the things there's still money in, they tell me.

SOAMES: Who are they, Arnold?

ARNOLD: Why, people ... what's the matter now?

SOAMES: Nothing's the matter, I just don't like being fobbed off ... they have never told you anything of the kind. Shall I tell you why? Because *they* are all the people you've never asked about the questions that never interested you. *They* tell me you should buy Kaffirs. *They* tell me you should sell Oil. *They* tell you there's money in tobacco. All lies, my friend.

ARNOLD: Well, for heaven's sake, Harry, what do you want me to do for you?

SOAMES: Now you're talking ... I want my old job back on the Arnold Holt Trust.

ARNOLD: You want what?

SOAMES: Don't you see, Arnold, it's my only chance. If you ever owed me anything, this is how you can repay a hundredfold. Just let me see that you have faith in me, that you're willing to give me another chance.

ARNOLD: Well, Harry, I'd like to do it, only I don't quite know how my associates would feel. I have a duty to them too, you know.

SOAMES: Sure I understand. I didn't think it would work, but it was worth trying. You see, I'm pretty desperate, so desperate that I had to come crawling to the great Arnold Holt himself, who hasn't exactly got the reputation in these parts of helping lame dogs over stiles.

ARNOLD: You've no right to talk like that... I said I'd do anything I can within reason, and I will. But frankly, I think you'd be making a mistake to try and come back in the city... there are lots of other fields open to a man of your ability.

SOAMES: You forget I'm a gaolbird.

ARNOLD: Oh no, I don't, you don't give me much opportunity to forget that. But you could go away somewhere, change your name if necessary.

SOAMES: Sure, I might call myself Phelps, like my wife does nowadays. Mabel Phelps, that's how I have to write to her.

ARNOLD: Look, Harry, all this self-pity won't get you anywhere, nor will that stuff. You'd better lay off it. Why don't you go away and think all this over ... and come and lunch with me one day next week?

(*He offers* SOAMES *his hand.* SOAMES *ignores it.*)

SOAMES: All right. Which day?

ARNOLD: Well, now, let me see ... Miss Perry has my engagement book, we'd better ask her. Tell you what, you ring me up to-morrow morning, there's a good fellow, and we'll fix a day. By the way, how are you off for cash?

SOAMES: I'm all right, thanks. I'm fine. I'll certainly call you, and if by any remote chance you're too busy next week, just leave a message with the great Miss Perry. I'll understand. You can put that ruler away now. You haven't drawn a straight line for years. (*He goes out.*)

FROM **The Master Builder**

By HENRIK IBSEN,
translated *By* EDMUND GOSSE and
WILLIAM ARCHER

In the notes introducing the scene from
A Doll's House which appears in Part One of
this book, it was pointed out how very
"actable" so much of Ibsen remains to this
day. The scene that follows, from Act I of
The Master Builder, further confirms this.
(It also offers an interesting comparison with
the situation in the scene from *Edward, My
Son*, just given.)

Other good acting exercises in this play
are the Solness-Dr. Herdal scene that occurs
later in Act I, and the several scenes through-
out the play between Solness and Hilda.

Brovik is a white-haired old man in a
threadbare coat. His employer, Solness—
"The Master Builder"—is a vigorous man in
his middle years; his clothes, though casual
in style, are expensively tailored.

BROVIK (*Lowering his voice a little*): I don't want
the poor children to know how ill I am.

SOLNESS: Yes, you've been looking very poorly of late.

BROVIK: It will soon be all over with me. My strength is ebbing from day to day.

SOLNESS: Won't you sit down?

BROVIK: Thanks—may I?

SOLNESS (*Placing the armchair more conveniently*): Here—take this chair. —And now?

BROVIK (*Has seated himself with difficulty*): Well, you see, it's about Ragnar. That's what weighs most upon me. What is to become of him?

SOLNESS: Of course your son will stay with me as long as ever he likes.

BROVIK: But that's just what he doesn't like. He feels that he can't stay any longer.

SOLNESS: Why, I should say he was very well off here. But if he wants a rise, I shouldn't object to—

BROVIK: No, no! It's not *that*. (*Impatiently*): But sooner or later he, too, must have a chance of doing something on his own account.

SOLNESS (*Without looking at him*): Do you think that Ragnar has quite talent enough to stand alone?

BROVIK: No, that's just the heart-breaking part of

it—I've begun to have my doubts about the boy. For you've never said so much as—as one encouraging word about him. And yet I can't help thinking there must be something in him—he can't possibly be without talent.

SOLNESS: Well, but he has learnt nothing—nothing thoroughly, I mean. Except, of course, to draw.

BROVIK (*Looks at him with covert hatred, and says hoarsely*): You had learned little enough of the business when you were in my employment. But that didn't prevent you from setting to work— (*Breathing with difficulty*): —and pushing your way up, and taking the wind out of my sails—mine, and other people's.

SOLNESS: Yes, you see—circumstances favored me.

BROVIK: You're right there. Everything favored you. But then how can you have the heart to let me go to my grave—without having seen what Ragnar is fit for? And of course I'm anxious to see them married, too—before I go.

SOLNESS (*Sharply*): Is it she who wishes it?

BROVIK: Not Kaia so much as Ragnar—he talks about it every day. (*Appealingly*): You must—you *must* help him to get some independent work now! I *must* see something that the lad has done. Do you hear?

SOLNESS (*Peevishly*): You can't expect me to drag commissions down from the moon for him!

BROVIK: He has the chance of a capital commission at this very moment. A big bit of work.

SOLNESS: (*Uneasily, startled*): Has he?

BROVIK: If *you* would give your consent.

SOLNESS: What sort of work do you mean?

BROVIK (*With some hesitation*): He can have the building of that villa out at Lövstrand.

SOLNESS: That! Why, I'm going to build that myself!

BROVIK: Oh, you don't much care about doing it.

SOLNESS (*Flaring up*): Don't care! I! Who dares to say that?

BROVIK: You said so yourself just now.

SOLNESS: Oh, never mind what I say. —Would they give Ragnar the building of that villa?

BROVIK: Yes. You see, he knows the family. And then—just for the fun of the thing—he's made drawings and estimates and so forth—

SOLNESS: Are they pleased with the drawings? The people who've got to live in the house?

BROVIK: Yes. If you would only look through them and approve of them—

SOLNESS: Then they would let Ragnar build their home for them?

BROVIK: They were immensely pleased with his idea. They thought it exceedingly original, they said.

SOLNESS: Oho! Original! Not the old-fashioned stuff that *I'm* in the habit of turning out.

BROVIK: It seemed to them *different*.

SOLNESS (*With suppressed irritation*): So it was to see Ragnar that they came here—whilst I was out!

BROVIK: They came to call upon you—and at the same time to ask whether you would mind retiring—

SOLNESS (*Angrily*): Retire? I?

BROVIK: In case you thought that Ragnar's drawings—

SOLNESS: I? Retire in favor of your son?

BROVIK: Retire from the agreement, they meant.

SOLNESS: Oh, it comes to the same thing. (*Laughs angrily.*) So that's it, is it? Halvard Solness is to see about retiring now! To make room for younger men! For the very youngest, perhaps! He's got to make room! Room! Room!

BROVIK: Why, good heavens! There's surely room for more than one single man—

SOLNESS: Oh, there's not so very much room to spare either. But be that as it may—I will never retire! I will never give way to anybody! Never of my own free will. Never in this world will I do *that!*

BROVIK (*Rises with difficulty*): Then I am to pass out of life without any certainty? Without a gleam of happiness? Without any faith or trust in Ragnar? Without having seen a single piece of work of his doing? Is that to be the way of it?

SOLNESS (*Turns half aside, and mutters*): H'm—don't ask more just now.

BROVIK: But answer me this one thing. Am I to pass out of life in such utter poverty?

SOLNESS (*Seems to struggle with himself; finally he says in a low but firm voice*): You must pass out of life as best you can.

BROVIK: Then be it so. (*He goes up the room.*)

SOLNESS (*Following him, half in desperation*): Don't you understand that I *cannot* help it? I am what I am, and I can't change my nature!

BROVIK: No, no; you evidently can't. (*Reels and supports himself against the sofa-table.*) May I have a glass of water?

SOLNESS: By all means. (*Fills a glass and hands it to him.*)

BROVIK: Thanks.

(*He drinks and puts the glass down again.* SOLNESS *goes up and opens the door of the draughtsmen's office.*)

SOLNESS: Ragnar—you must come and take your father home.

FROM **A Woman of No Importance**

By OSCAR WILDE

An actor is faced with no greater challenge, perhaps, than being required to spout epigrams, for epigrammatic dialogue seldom offers him enough points at which he can merge his own personality with his character's. Epigrams are written purely for the audience's intellectual delight. They do not reveal motivation. They do not supply strong objectives around which the actor can play. They are seldom even very useful for developing and refining characterization, since it is really the playwright's voice that is speaking them rather than the character's.

Actors cast in epigrammatic plays such as Wilde's *A Woman of No Importance* must ultimately find their own answers to making the dialogue believable to themselves and to the audience. Certainly scenes such as the following are excellent exercises in truthful talking and listening.

The scene opens Act III. Gerald Arbuthnot is a young man, Lord Illingworth a man of middle age. The former is naive, the latter utterly sophisticated. (Lord Illingworth also happens to be Gerald's father—but Gerald is unaware of this fact at this point in the play.)

ILLINGWORTH: Thoroughly sensible woman, your mother, Gerald. I knew she would come round in the end.

GERALD: My mother is awfully conscientious, Lord Illingworth, and I know she doesn't think I am educated enough to be your secretary. She is perfectly right, too. I was fearfully idle when I was at school, and I couldn't pass an examination now to save my life.

ILLINGWORTH: My dear Gerald, examinations are of no value whatsoever. If a man is a gentleman, he knows quite enough, and if he is not a gentleman, whatever he knows is bad for him.

GERALD: But I am so ignorant of the world, Lord Illingworth.

ILLINGWORTH: Don't be afraid, Gerald. Remember that you've got on your side the most wonderful thing in the world—youth! There is nothing like youth. The middle-aged are mortgaged to Life. The old are in Life's lumber-room. But youth is the Lord of Life. Youth has a kingdom waiting for it. Every one is born a king, and most people die in exile, like most kings. To win back my youth, Gerald, there is nothing I wouldn't do—except take exercise, get up early, or be a useful member of the community.

GERALD: But you don't call yourself old, Lord Illingworth?

ILLINGWORTH: I am old enough to be your father, Gerald.

GERALD: I don't remember my father; he died years ago.

ILLINGWORTH: So Lady Hunstanton told me.

GERALD: It is very curious, my mother never talks to me about my father. I sometimes think she must have married beneath her.

ILLINGWORTH (*Winces slightly*): Really? (*Goes over and puts his hand on* GERALD's *shoulder.*) You have missed not having a father, I suppose, Gerald?

GERALD: Oh, no; my mother has been so good to me. No one ever had such a mother as I have had.

ILLINGWORTH: I am quite sure of that. Still I should imagine that most mothers don't quite understand their sons. Don't realise, I mean, that a son has ambitions, a desire to see life, to make himself a name. After all, Gerald, you couldn't be expected to pass all your life in such a hole as Wrockley, could you?

GERALD: Oh, no! It would be dreadful!

ILLINGWORTH: A mother's love is very touching, of course, but it is often curiously selfish. I mean, there is a good deal of selfishness in it.

GERALD (*Slowly*): I suppose there is.

ILLINGWORTH: Your mother is a thoroughly good woman. But good women have such limited views of life, their horizon is so small, their interests are so petty, aren't they?

GERALD: They are awfully interested, certainly, in things we don't care much about.

ILLINGWORTH: I suppose your mother is very religious, and that sort of thing.

GERALD: Oh, yes, she's always going to church.

ILLINGWORTH: Ah! she is not modern, and to be modern is the only thing worth being now-a-days. You want to be modern, don't you, Gerald? You want to know life as it really is. Not to be put off with any old-fashioned theories about life. Well, what you have to do at present is simply to fit yourself for the best society. A man who can dominate a London dinner-table can dominate the world. The future belongs to the dandy. It is the exquisites who are going to rule.

GERALD: I should like to wear nice things awfully, but I have always been told that a man should not think too much about his clothes.

ILLINGWORTH: People now-a-days are so absolutely superficial that they don't understand the philosophy of the superficial. By the way, Gerald, you should learn how to tie your tie better. Sentiment is all very well for the button-hole. But the essential thing for a necktie is style. A well-tied tie is the first serious step in life.

GERALD (*Laughing*): I might be able to learn how to tie a tie, Lord Illingworth, but I should never be able to talk as you do. I don't know how to talk.

ILLINGWORTH: Oh! talk to every woman as if you loved her, and to every man as if he bored you, and at the end of your first season you will have the reputation of possessing the most perfect social tact.

GERALD: But it is very difficult to get into society, isn't it?

ILLINGWORTH: To get into the best society, now-a-days, one has either to feed people, amuse people, or shock people—that is all.

GERALD: I suppose society is wonderfully delightful!

ILLINGWORTH: To be in it is merely a bore. But to be out of it simply a tragedy. Society is a necessary thing. No man has any real success in this world unless he has got women to back him, and women rule society. If you have not got women on your side you are quite over. You might as well be a barrister, or a stockbroker, or a journalist at once.

GERALD: It is very difficult to understand women, is it not?

ILLINGWORTH: You should never try to understand them. Women are pictures. Men are problems. If you want to know what a woman really means—which, by the way, is always a dangerous thing to do—look at her, don't listen to her.

GERALD: But women are awfully clever, aren't they?

ILLINGWORTH: One should always tell them so. But, to the philosopher, my dear Gerald, women represent the triumph of matter over mind—just as men represent the triumph of mind over morals.

GERALD: How then can women have so much power as you say they have?

ILLINGWORTH: The history of women is the history of the worst form of tyranny the world has ever known. The tyranny of the weak over the strong. It is the only tyranny that lasts.

GERALD: But haven't women got a refining influence?

ILLINGWORTH: Nothing refines but the intellect.

GERALD: Still, there are many different kinds of women, aren't there?

ILLINGWORTH: Only two kinds in society: the plain and the coloured.

GERALD: But there are good women in society, aren't there?

ILLINGWORTH: Far too many.

GERALD: But do you think women shouldn't be good?

ILLINGWORTH: One should never tell them so, they'd all become good at once. Women are a fascinatingly wilful sex. Every woman is a rebel, and usually in wild revolt against herself.

GERALD: You have never been married, Lord Illingworth, have you?

ILLINGWORTH: Men marry because they are tired; women because they are curious. Both are disappointed.

GERALD: But don't you think one can be happy when one is married?

ILLINGWORTH: Perfectly happy. But the happiness of a married man, my dear Gerald, depends on the people he has not married.

GERALD: But if one is in love?

ILLINGWORTH: One should always be in love. That is the reason one should never marry.

GERALD: Love is a very wonderful thing, isn't it?

ILLINGWORTH: When one is in love one begins by deceiving oneself. And one ends by deceiving others. That is what the world calls a romance. But a really *grande passion* is comparatively rare now-a-days. It is the privilege of people who have nothing to do. That is the one use of the idle classes in a country, and the only possible explanation of us Harfords.

GERALD: Harfords, Lord Illingworth?

ILLINGWORTH: That is my family name. You should study the Peerage, Gerald. It is the one book a young man about town should know thoroughly, and it is the best thing in fiction the English have ever done.

The Seventh Seal

By INGMAR BERGMAN,
translated *By* LARS MALMSTROM and
DAVID KUSHNER

It is a far cry from the superficiality of Oscar Wilde to the dark psychological probings of film-maker Ingmar Bergman; yet the scene that follows is almost as great a challenge as the one above. Like the Wilde scene, it offers only scanty clues to characterization and motivation; the truthful talking and listening of the actors is essential if the scene is to work, for it has little momentum of its own. (And don't be misled by the scene's brevity and simple language into thinking it's a snap to play; it isn't.)

The film is set in the middle ages. Jöns, a squire, enters a church, where he finds a man at work on an elaborate fresco.

JÖNS: What is this supposed to represent?

PAINTER: The Dance of Death.

JÖNS: And that one is Death?

PAINTER: Yes, he dances off with all of them.

JÖNS: Why do you paint such nonsense?

PAINTER: I thought it would serve to remind people that they must die.

JÖNS: Well, it's not going to make them feel any happier.

PAINTER: Why should one always make people happy? It might not be a bad idea to scare them a little once in a while.

JÖNS: Then they'll close their eyes and refuse to look at your painting.

PAINTER: Oh, they'll look. A skull is almost more interesting than a naked woman.

JÖNS: If you do scare them...

PAINTER: They'll think.

JÖNS: And if they think...

PAINTER: They'll become still more scared.

JÖNS: And then they'll run right into the arms of the priests.

PAINTER: That's not my business.

JÖNS: You're only painting your Dance of Death.

PAINTER: I'm only painting things as they are. Everyone else can do as he likes.

JÖNS: Just think how some people will curse you.

PAINTER: Maybe. But then I'll paint something amusing for them to look at. I have to make a living— at least until the plague takes me.

JÖNS: The plague. That sounds horrible.

PAINTER: You should see the boils on a diseased man's throat. You should see how his body shrivels up so that his legs look like knotted strings—like the man I've painted over there.
(The PAINTER *points with his brush.* JÖNS *sees a small human form writhing in the grass, its eyes turned upward in a frenzied look of horror and pain.*)

JÖNS: That looks terrible.

PAINTER: It certainly does. He tries to rip out the boil, he bites his hands, tears his veins open with his fingernails and his screams can be heard everywhere. Does that scare you?

JÖNS: Scare? Me? You don't know me. What are the horrors you've painted over there?

PAINTER: The remarkable thing is that the poor creatures think the pestilence is the Lord's punishment. Mobs of people who call themselves Slaves of

Sin are swarming over the country, flagellating themselves and others, all for the glory of God.

JÖNS: Do they really whip themselves?

PAINTER: Yes, it's a terrible sight. I crawl into a ditch and hide when they pass by.

JÖNS: Do you have any brandy? I've been drinking water all day and it's made me as thirsty as a camel in the desert.

PAINTER: I think I frightened you after all.

The Waltz of the Toreadors

By JEAN ANOUILH,
translated *By* LUCIENNE HILL

Plays that are elegant and graceful and delicate, as a rule, find little favor with audiences in the twentieth century; such plays often prove too fragile for success in the commercial theater. A conspicuous exception are the plays of Jean Anouilh; and perhaps his plays are successful because for all their delicacy, they have a toughness about them. Their characters are imbued with strong sinews and earthy sense.

General St. Pé, the hero of *The Waltz of the Toreadors*, is a sensitive, gentle lecher; his wife is a fragile, bedridden harridan. As this scene in Act III begins, Doctor Bonfant, the general's close friend, is just coming into the general's study, having examined Mme. St. Pé. (There is another good scene between the same characters at the opening of Act II, Scene 1; and for an actor and actress, Act II, Scene 2 is one long dialogue between the general and his impossible wife.)

DOCTOR: I have just taken her blood pressure. She's as right as rain. She's had a bad fright, that's all.

GENERAL: So did I.

DOCTOR: So did I, my friend. The moment your maid appeared and said to come at once, I guessed Madam was choking.

GENERAL: What did she say?

DOCTOR: Who? Your maid?

GENERAL: My wife.

DOCTOR: My poor friend, she seems to think it quite in order that you should want to do away with her. Murder is the regular concomitant of passion at the opera. She submits gracefully, biding her time, no doubt, and feeling vaguely flattered: she is more than ever convinced that you are a pair of sublime and star-crossed lovers.

GENERAL: Oh, the idiocy of it! Will she never understand that she quite simply bores me?

DOCTOR: I'm afraid you will have to face up to it, General. Never.

GENERAL: But, dear God, that can't be all there is to life! Why did no one ever warn me? Everybody looks happy round about me, and content. How do they do it, damn them—how do they manage not to suffer? What is their password? Let them tell it me, at once. I've no more time to wait.

DOCTOR: My dear old friend, I think that is a question one must ask oneself when one is very much younger.

GENERAL (*Yelling*): I *am* young! Lieutenant St. Pé! I decline all other rank! It's nothing but a booby trap! I see it now. (*Suddenly*): Doctor, has medicine not discovered anything to put the clock back seventeen years?

DOCTOR: Nothing so far.

GENERAL: Are you sure?

DOCTOR: It would surely have been mentioned in certain ... specialist publications.

GENERAL: Are you aware of what's going on? Mlle. de Ste.-Euverte and my secretary have gone out for a walk. They've been away nearly two hours.

DOCTOR: Nothing very odd about that. You were closeted with your wife. Your explanations bode fair to going on forever. I expect they simply decided to go for a short stroll while they were waiting.

GENERAL: A curious misunderstanding arose between the two of them this morning. Then they left, with their little fingers linked, so the maid tells me. Does that strike you as normal too? As for my daughters, who were enamoured of our hero—they have gone as well, leaving this letter on the table, together with their fake jewelry wrapped up in tissue paper. (*He pulls a letter out of his pocket.*) "We are too unhappy. He is in love with another. We prefer to die"—(two more of them, it's all the rage in this house)—"Tell Mme. Dupont-Fredaine not to go on with our dresses." Among other primordial virtues their mother has imbued them with a solid notion of economy.

DOCTOR: Good Heavens, and haven't they come home yet?

GENERAL: I sent the gardener in search of them. They must be down by the pond, dabbling their feet in the water. They're far too plain to kill themselves. Everything is tumbling about my ears! Dear God, how will it all end?

DOCTOR: As in real life—or in the theatre, in the days when plays *were* plays—a contrived dénouement, not too gloomy on the face of it, and which doesn't really fool a soul, and then a little later—curtain. I speak for myself as well as you. Your blood pressure's up to two hundred and fifty and my gall bladder is a bag of stones. Make way for the young! May they commit the self-same follies and die of the same diseases.

GENERAL: But I love her, Doctor, and I am young!

FROM # The Two Gentlemen of Verona

By WILLIAM SHAKESPEARE

The neglect of Shakespeare's *Cymbeline* is easier to understand than the neglect of *The Two Gentlemen of Verona*. The two gentlemen, Valentine and Proteus, and the ladies they love, Julia and Sylvia, are surely appealing characters, and the play's clowns, Speed and Launce, are among Shakespeare's happiest rustic characters.

Would-be comedians and character men alike should enjoy playing the following scene between Speed, servant to Valentine, and Launce, servant to Proteus. It occurs in Act III, Scene 1.

SPEED: How now, Signior Launce! what news with your mastership?

LAUNCE: With my master's ship? why, it is at sea.

SPEED: Well, your old vice still; mistake the word. What news, then, in your paper?

LAUNCE: The blackest news that ever thou heardest.

SPEED: Why, man, how black?

LAUNCE: Why, as black as ink.

SPEED: Let me read them.

LAUNCE: Fie on thee, jolt-head! thou canst not read.

SPEED: Thou liest; I can.

LAUNCE: I will try thee. Tell me this: who begot thee?

SPEED: Marry, the son of my grandfather.

LAUNCE: O illiterate loiterer! it was the son of thy grandmother: this proves that thou canst not read.

SPEED: Come, fool, come; try me in thy paper.

LAUNCE: There; and Saint Nicholas be thy speed!

SPEED (*Reads*): 'Imprimis: She can milk.'

LAUNCE: Ay, that she can.

SPEED: 'Item: She brews good ale.'

LAUNCE: And thereof comes the proverb: 'Blessing of your heart, you brew good ale.'

SPEED: 'Item: She can sew.'

LAUNCE: That's as much as to say, Can she so?

SPEED: 'Item: She can knit!'

LAUNCE: What need a man care for a stock with a wench, when she can knit him a stock?

SPEED: 'Item: She can wash and scour.'

LAUNCE: A special virtue; for then she need not be washed and scoured.

SPEED: 'Item: She can spin.'

LAUNCE: Then may I set the world on wheels, when she can spin for her living.

SPEED: 'Item: She hath many nameless virtues.'

LAUNCE: That's as much as to say, bastard virtues; that, indeed, know not their fathers and therefore have no names.

SPEED: 'Here follow her vices.'

LAUNCE: Close at the heels of her virtues.

SPEED: 'Item: She is not to be kissed fasting, in respect of her breath.'

LAUNCE: Well, that fault may be mended with a breakfast. Read on.

SPEED: 'Item: She hath a sweet mouth.'

LAUNCE: That makes amends for her sour breath.

SPEED: 'Item: She doth talk in her sleep.'

LAUNCE: It's no matter for that, so she sleep not in her talk.

SPEED: 'Item: She is slow in words.'

LAUNCE: O villain, that set this down among her vices! To be slow in words is a woman's only virtue: I pray thee, out with't, and place it for her chief virtue.

SPEED: 'Item: She is proud.'

LAUNCE: Out with that too; it was Eve's legacy, and cannot be ta'en from her.

SPEED: 'Item: She hath no teeth.'

LAUNCE: I care not for that neither, because I love crusts.

SPEED: 'Item: She is curst.'

LAUNCE: Well, the best is, she hath no teeth to bite.

SPEED: 'Item: She will often praise her liquor.'

LAUNCE: If her liquor be good, she shall: if she will not, I will; for good things should be praised.

SPEED: 'Item: She is too liberal.'

LAUNCE: Of her tongue she cannot, for that's writ

down she is slow of; of her purse she shall not, for
that I'll keep shut; now, of another thing she may,
and that cannot I help. Well, proceed.

SPEED: 'Item: She hath more hair than wit, and
more faults than hairs, and more wealth than faults.'

LAUNCE: Stop there; I'll have her: she was mine
and not mine, twice or thrice in that last article.
Rehearse that once more.

SPEED: 'Item: She hath more hair than wit,'—

LAUNCE: More hair than wit? It may be: I'll prove
it. The cover of the salt hides the salt, and therefore
it is more than the salt; the hair that covers the wit
is more than the wit, for the greater hides the less.
What's next?

SPEED: 'And more faults than hairs,'—

LAUNCE: That's monstrous: O, that that were out!

SPEED: 'And more wealth than faults.'

LAUNCE: Why, that word makes the faults gracious.
Well, I'll have her: and if it be a match, as nothing
is impossible—

SPEED: What then?

LAUNCE: Why, then will I tell thee—that thy master
stays for thee at the North-gate.

SPEED: For me?

LAUNCE: For thee! ay, who art thou? he hath stayed for a better man than thee.

SPEED: And must I go to him?

LAUNCE: Thou must run to him, for thou hast stayed so long that going will scarce serve the turn.

SPEED: Why didst not tell me sooner? pox of your love-letters! (*He goes.*)

LAUNCE: Now will he be swinged for reading my letter; an unmannerly slave, that will thrust himself into secrets! I'll after, to rejoice in the boy's correction. (*He goes.*)

Daisy Miller

By HENRY JAMES

Although he regarded himself as a writer primarily of prose fiction, for which, of course, he became justly famous, Henry James was long intrigued with the theater, and wrote some fifteen plays. Of these, the most interesting, from both a literary and a dramatic point of view, is his dramatization of his own short novel, *Daisy Miller*.

In this scene from Act II, Giacomo Giovanelli, who is intent upon marrying the title character for her fortune, meets by appointment with Eugenio, who is to help arrange the matter.

GIOVANELLI (*Cautious, looking round him*): You might have proposed meeting in some less conspicuous spot!

EUGENIO: In the Coliseum, at midnight? My dear sir, we should be much more compromised if we were discovered there!

GIOVANELLI: Oh, if you count upon our being discovered! . . .

EUGENIO: There is nothing so unnatural in our having a little conversation. One should never be ashamed of an accomplice!

GIOVANELLI (*With a grimace, disgusted*): Don't speak of accomplices: as if we were concocting a crime!

EUGENIO: What makes it a work of merit is my conviction that you are a perfect gentleman. If it hadn't been for that, I never should have presented you to my family.

GIOVANELLI: Your family? You speak as if, in marrying the girl, I should become your brother-in-law.

EUGENIO: We shall certainly be united by a very peculiar tie!

GIOVANELLI: United—united? I don't know about that! After my marriage, I shall travel without a courier. (*Smiling*): It will be less expensive!

EUGENIO: In the event you speak of, I myself hardly expect to remain in the ranks. I have seen too many campaigns: I shall retire on my pension. You look as if you did not understand me.

GIOVANELLI: Perfectly. You expect the good Mrs. Miller to make you comfortable for the rest of your days.

EUGENIO: What I expect of the good Mrs. Miller is one thing; what I expect of you is another: and on that point we had better be perfectly clear. It was to insure perfect clearness that I proposed this little conference, which you refused to allow to take place either in your own lodgings or in some comfortable café. Oh, I know you had your reasons! You don't exhibit your little interior; and though I know a good deal about you, I don't know where you live. It doesn't matter, I don't want to know: it's enough for me that I can always find you here, amid the music and the flowers. But I can't exactly make out why you wouldn't meet me at a café. I would gladly have paid for a glass of beer.

GIOVANELLI: It was just your beer that I was afraid of! I never touch the beastly stuff.

EUGENIO: Ah, if you drink nothing but champagne, no wonder you are looking for an heiress! But before I help you to one, let me give you a word of advice. Make the best of me, if you wish me to make the best of you. I was determined to do that when I presented you to the two most amiable women in the world.

GIOVANELLI: I must protest against your theory that you presented me. I met Mrs. Miller at a party, as any gentleman might have done.

EUGENIO: You met her at a party, precisely; but unless I wish it, Mrs. Miller doesn't go to a party! I let you know she was to be there, and I advised you how to proceed. For the last three weeks I have done nothing but arrange little accidents, little surprises, little occasions, of which I will do you the justice to say that you have taken excellent advantage. But the time has come when I must remind you that I have not done all this from mere admiration of your distinguished appearance. I wish your success to be *my* success!

GIOVANELLI (*Pleased, with a certain simplicity*): I am glad to hear you talk about my success!

EUGENIO: Oh, there's a good deal to be said about it! Have you ever been to the circus?

GIOVANELLI: I don't see what that has to do with it?

EUGENIO: You've seen the bareback rider turn a somersault through the paper hoops? It's a very pretty feat, and it brings him great applause; but half the effect depends upon the poor devil—whom no one notices—who is perched upon the edge of the ring. If he didn't hold the hoop with a great deal of skill, the bareback rider would simply come down on his nose. You turn your little somersaults, Signor Cavaliere, and my young lady claps her hands; but all the while *I'm* holding the hoop!

GIOVANELLI: If I'm not mistaken, that office, at the circus, is usually performed by the clown.

EUGENIO: Take very good care, or you'll have a fall!

GIOVANELLI: I suppose you want to be paid for your trouble.

EUGENIO: The point isn't that I want to be paid; that goes without saying! But I want to be paid handsomely.

GIOVANELLI: What do you call handsomely?

EUGENIO: A commission proportionate to the fortune of the young lady. I know something about that. I have in my pocket (*slapping his side*) the letter of credit of the Signora. She lets me carry it—for safety's sake!

GIOVANELLI: Poor Signora! It's a strange game we are playing!

EUGENIO (*Looking at him a moment*): Oh, if you doubt of the purity of your motives, you have only to say so. You swore to me that you adored my young lady.

GIOVANELLI: She's an angel, and I worship the ground she treads on. That makes me wonder whether I couldn't get on without you.

EUGENIO (*Dryly*): Try it and see. I have only to say the word, and Mrs. Miller will start to-morrow for the north.

GIOVANELLI: And if you don't say the word, that's another thing you want to be paid for! It mounts up very fast.

EUGENIO: It mounts up to fifty thousand francs, to be handed to me six months after you are married.

GIOVANELLI: Fifty thousand francs?

EUGENIO: The family exchequer will never miss them. Besides, I give you six months. You sign a little note, "for value received."

GIOVANELLI: And if the marriage—if the marriage—

EUGENIO: If the marriage comes to grief, I burn up the note.

GIOVANELLI: How can I be sure of that?

EUGENIO: By having already perceived that I'm not an idiot. If you don't marry, you can't pay: I need no one to tell me that. But I intend you *shall* marry.

GIOVANELLI (*Satirical*): It's uncommonly good of you! After all, I haven't a squint!

EUGENIO: I picked you out for your good looks; and you're so tremendously fascinating that even when I lose patience with your want of everything else I can't afford to sacrifice you. Your prospects are now very good. The estimable mother—

GIOVANELLI: The estimable mother believes me to be already engaged to her daughter. It shows how much she knows about it!

EUGENIO: No, you are not engaged, but you will be, next week. You have rather too many flowers there, by the way: you overdo it a little. (*Pointing to* GIOVANELLI'*s buttonhole.*)

GIOVANELLI: So long as you pay for them, the more the better! How far will it carry me to be engaged? Mr. Miller can hardly be such a fool as his wife.

EUGENIO (*Stroking his moustache*): Mr. Miller?

GIOVANELLI: The mysterious father, in that unpronounceable town! He must be a man of energy, to have made such a fortune, and the idea of his energy haunts me!

EUGENIO: That's because you've got none yourself.

GIOVANELLI: I don't pretend to that; I only pretend to—a—

EUGENIO: To be fascinating, I know! But you're afraid the papa won't see it.

GIOVANELLI: I don't exactly see why he should set his heart on a Roman son-in-law.

EUGENIO: It's your business to produce that miracle!

GIOVANELLI: By making the girl talked about? My respect for her is in proportion to the confidence she shows me. That confidence is unlimited.

EUGENIO: Oh, unlimited! I have never seen anything like that confidence; and if out of such a piece of cloth as that you can't cut a coat—

GIOVANELLI: I never pretended to be a tailor! And you must not forget that I have a rival.

EUGENIO: Forget it? I regard it as a particularly gratifying fact. If you didn't have a rival I should have very small hopes of you.

GIOVANELLI: I confess I don't follow you. The young lady's confidence in Mr. Winterbourne is at least equal to her confidence in me.

EUGENIO: Ah, but *his* confidence in the young lady? That's another affair! He thinks she goes too far. He's an American, like herself; but there are Americans and Americans, and when they take it into their heads to open their eyes they open them very wide.

GIOVANELLI: If you mean that this American's a donkey, I see no reason to differ with you.

EUGENIO: Leave him to me. I've got a stick to beat him with!

GIOVANELLI: You make me shiver a little! Do you mean to put him out of the way?

EUGENIO: I mean to put him out of the way. Ah, you can trust me! I don't carry a stiletto, and if you'll excuse me I won't describe my little plan. You'll tell me what you think of it when you have seen the results. The great feature is simply that Miss Daisy, seeing herself abandoned—

GIOVANELLI: Will look about her for a consoler? Ah, consolation is a specialty of mine, and if you give me a chance to console I think I shall be safe.

EUGENIO: I shall go to work on the spot!
(*He takes out his pocket-book, from which he extracts a small folded paper, holding it up a moment before* GIOVANELLI.)

EUGENIO: Put your name to that, and send it back to me by post.

GIOVANELLI (*Reading the paper with a little grimace*): Fifty thousand! Fifty thousand is steep.

EUGENIO: Signor Cavaliere, the letter of credit is for half a million!

GIOVANELLI (*Pocketing the paper*): Well, give me a chance to console—give me a chance to console!

FROM **The Barber of Seville**

By PIERRE-AUGUSTIN CARON DE BEAUMARCHAIS, translated *By* WALLACE FOWLIE

That neither content nor historical period alone is sufficient to determine the correct style of playing a given scene is immediately apparent when one compares this scene from Beaumarchais' famous comedy with the scene from *Daisy Miller* given above and with the scene from Richard Brinsley Sheridan's *The Duenna*, which follows. Sheridan was Beaumarchais' contemporary; yet their plays take place in very different worlds. Like the *Daisy Miller* scene, this one concerns a patrician master in pursuit of a lady being abetted by a coarser but shrewder employee; but again, what a difference in the world of the play!

The Count, who is Figaro's master, has assumed a disguise.

FIGARO: My lord, I don't need to look any farther for the motives of your masquerade. You are making love in perspective.

COUNT: Now you know. If you ever talk...

FIGARO: Me, talk? I won't use any high-sounding phrases of honor and devotion, which are always being abused, to reassure you. Just one word. My own interests will answer for me. Weigh everything in that balance, and...

COUNT: Very well. You should know that six months ago, by chance, in the Prado I met a young girl of such beauty... You have just seen her. I searched for her everywhere in Madrid. Just a few days ago I discovered that her name is Rosine, that she is of noble blood, an orphan, and married to an old physician of this city, called Bartholo.

FIGARO: A pretty bird, but hard to get out of the nest! Who told you she is the doctor's wife?

COUNT: Everyone.

FIGARO: That's a story he made up when he came from Madrid, in order to trick all suitors and get rid of them. She is only his ward, but soon...

COUNT (*Ardently*): Never! What news! I was determined to dare everything to tell her my regrets, and now I learn she is free! There's not a moment to lose. I must make her love me and rescue her from the unworthy marriage they are planning. Do you know this guardian?

FIGARO: As well as my mother.

COUNT: What sort of man is he?

FIGARO (*Excitedly*): He's a handsome, fat, short, young, old man, dapple gray, crafty, clean-shaven, blasé, peeping, prying, scolding, moaning, all at once.

COUNT (*Impatiently*): I've seen him. What's his character?

FIGARO: Brutal, miserly, passionate, and absurdly jealous of his ward who hates him with a terrible hate.

COUNT: So, his ability to please is...

FIGARO: Zero.

COUNT: Good! What about his honesty?

FIGARO: Just enough honesty not to be hanged.

COUNT: Still better. To punish a rascal while finding my happiness...

FIGARO: Is to do a public and a private good. In truth, a masterpiece of morality, my lord!

COUNT: You say that fear of suitors makes him keep his door locked?

FIGARO: Locked to everyone. If he could stop up the cracks...

COUNT: The devil! That's too bad. Do you have access to the house?

FIGARO: Of course I do! The house where I live belongs to the doctor, and he lodges me there free.

COUNT: I see!

FIGARO: And in gratitude, I promise him ten pistoles a year, also free.

COUNT (*Impatient*): Are you his tenant?

FIGARO: Much more. His barber, his surgeon, his apothecary. There is not a stroke of the razor, of the lancet, or of the syringe in his house which does not come from the hand of your servant.

COUNT (*Embraces him*): Ah, Figaro, dear friend, you will be my liberator, my guardian angel.

FIGARO: Well! My usefulness has shortened the distances between us. Talk to me of men with a passion!

COUNT: Lucky Figaro! You are going to see my Rosine. You will see her! Do you realize your good fortune?

FIGARO: That's the way a lover talks. I'm not in love with her. I wish you could take my place.

COUNT: If we could only get rid of all the guards!

FIGARO: That's what I was thinking of.

COUNT: Just for one day.

FIGARO: By inducing people to look out for their own interests, we'll keep them from interfering with the interests of others.

COUNT: That's right. So?

FIGARO (*Reflects*): I am wondering whether the art of pharmacy will not furnish some innocent means...

COUNT: Scoundrel!

FIGARO: I don't intend to hurt them. They all need my cane. It's a question of how to treat them all at once.

COUNT: But this doctor may grow suspicious.

FIGARO: We'll have to work so fast that there will be no time for suspicion. I have an idea. The regiment of the heir apparent has just come to the city.

COUNT: The colonel is one of my friends.

FIGARO: Good. Go to the doctor's house in a soldier's uniform, with a billet. He will have to give you lodging. I will take care of the rest.

COUNT: Excellent!

FIGARO: It would be a good idea if you were a bit... tipsy...

COUNT: Why?

FIGARO: And treat him unceremoniously. A little intoxication would make you unreasonable...

COUNT: But why?

FIGARO: So that he will take no offense, and think you more in a hurry to go to bed than to carry on intrigues in his house.

COUNT: A superb plan! But why aren't you in it?

FIGARO: Me? We'll be lucky if he doesn't recognize you whom he has never seen. How could I introduce you afterward?

COUNT: You are right.

FIGARO: But perhaps you won't be able to act out that difficult part. A cavalier—drunk on wine...

COUNT: You underestimate me. (*Imitating the speech of a drunkard*): Isn't this the house of Doctor Bartholo, my friend?

FIGARO: Not bad, really. You should be a little more unsteady on your legs. (*With a more drunken voice*): Isn't this the house of ... ?

COUNT: I'm surprised at you. That's the vulgar drunkenness of the people.

FIGARO: It's the best kind. It's the drunkenness of pleasure.

FROM The Duenna

By RICHARD BRINSLEY SHERIDAN

Sheridan is most famous—and justly so—for *The Rivals* and *The School for Scandal*, and student actors looking for good scene material would do well to investigate those plays. Sheridan's less well known works are not without merit, however, as this scene from Act III, Scene 2 of his comic opera, *The Duenna*, indicates. (Also worth reading for student actors is Sheridan's three-act play, *The Critic*; though lacking in good two-person scenes, it is one of the most entertaining satires on the subject of theater ever written.)

As in the two scenes given immediately above, the dialogue here centers on the woman loved by one of the two men. They are Don Ferdinand and Isaac Mendoza; the scene is the New Piazza in Seville.

FERDINAND (*Alone*): Oh, how my fondness for this ungrateful girl has hurt my disposition.

ISAAC (*Entering; to himself*): So, I have her safe, and have only to find a priest to marry us. Antonio now may marry Clara, or not, if he pleases.

FERDINAND: What! what was that you said of Clara?

ISAAC: Oh, Ferdinand! my brother-in-law that shall be, who thought of meeting you?

FERDINAND: But what of Clara?

ISAAC: I'faith, you shall hear. This morning, as I was coming down, I met a pretty damzel, who told me her name was Clara d'Almanza, and begged my protection.

FERDINAND: How!

ISAAC: She said she had eloped from her father, Don Guzman, but that love for a young gentleman in Seville was the cause.

FERDINAND: O heavens! did she confess it!

ISAAC: Oh, yes, she confessed at once. But then, says she, my lover is not informed of my flight, nor suspects my intention.

FERDINAND (*Aside*): Dear creature! no more I did, indeed! Oh, I am the happiest fellow! (*Aloud*): Well, Isaac?

ISAAC: Why then she entreated me to find him out for her, and bring him to her.

FERDINAND: Good heavens, how lucky! Well, come along; let's lose no time. (*Pulling him.*)

ISAAC: Zooks! where are we to go?

FERDINAND: Why, did anything more pass?

ISAAC: Anything more! yes; the end on't was, that I was moved with her speeches, and complied with her desires.

FERDINAND: Well, and where is she?

ISAAC: Where is she! why, don't I tell you? I complied with her request, and left her safe in the arms of her lover.

FERDINAND: 'Sdeath, you trifle with me! —I have never seen her.

ISAAC: You! O Lud, no! how the devil should you? 'Twas Antonio she wanted; and with Antonio I left her.

FERDINAND (*Aside*): Hell and madness! (*Aloud*): What, Antonio d'Ercilla?

ISAAC: Aye, aye, the very man; and the best part of it was, he was shy of taking her at first. He talked a good deal about honour, and conscience, and deceiving some dear friend; but, Lord, we soon overruled that!

FERDINAND: You did!

ISAAC: Oh, yes, presently. —Such deceit! says he.

—Pish! says the lady, tricking is all fair in love. But then, my friend, says he. —Psha! damn your friend, says I. So, poor wretch, he has no chance. —No, no; he may hang himself as soon as he pleases.

FERDINAND (*Aside*): I must go, or I shall betray myself.

ISAAC: But stay, Ferdinand, you ha'n't heard the best of the joke.

FERDINAND: Curse on your joke!

ISAAC: Good lack! what's the matter now? I thought to have diverted you.

FERDINAND: Be racked! tortured! damned!

ISAAC: Why, sure you are not the poor devil of a lover, are you? —I'faith, as sure as can be, he is! This is a better joke than t'other. Ha! ha! ha!

FERDINAND: What! Do you laugh? you vile, mischievous varlet! (*Collars him.*) But that you're beneath my anger, I'd tear your heart out! (*Throws him from him.*)

ISAAC: Oh, mercy! here's usage for a brother-in-law.

FERDINAND: But, hark ye, rascal! tell me directly where these false friends are gone, or, by my soul— (*Draws.*)

ISAAC: For Heaven's sake, now, my dear brother-in-law, don't be in a rage! I'll recollect as well as I can.

FERDINAND: Be quick, then!

ISAAC: I will, I will! —but people's memories differ; some have a treacherous memory; now mine is a cowardly memory—it takes to its heels at sight of a drawn sword, it does, i'faith; and I could as soon fight as recollect.

FERDINAND: Zounds! tell me the truth, and I won't hurt you.

ISAAC: No, no, I know you won't, my dear brother-in-law; but that ill-looking thing there—

FERDINAND: What, then, you won't tell me?

ISAAC: Yes, yes, I will; I'll tell you all, upon my soul! —but why need you listen, sword in hand?

FERDINAND: Why, there. (*Puts up.*) Now.

ISAAC: Why, then, I believe they are gone to—that is, my friend Carlos told me, he had left Donna Clara—dear Ferdinand, keep your hands off—at the convent of St. Catharine.

FERDINAND: St. Catharine!

ISAAC: Yes; and that Antonio was to come to her there.

FERDINAND: Is this the truth?

ISAAC: It is, indeed; and all I know, as I hope for life!

FERDINAND: Well, coward, take your life! 'tis that false, dishonourable Antonio who shall feel my vengeance.

ISAAC: Aye, aye, kill him; cut his throat, and welcome.

FERDINAND: But, for Clara! infamy on her! she is not worth my resentment.

ISAAC: No more she is, my dear brother-in-law. I'faith, I would not be angry about her; she is not worth it, indeed.

FERDINAND: 'Tis false! she is worth the enmity of princes!

ISAAC: True, true, so she is; and I pity you exceedingly for having lost her.

FERDINAND: 'Sdeath, you rascal! how durst you talk of pitying me?

ISAAC: Oh, dear brother-in-law, I beg pardon! I don't pity you in the least, upon my soul!

FERDINAND: Get hence, fool, and provoke me no further; nothing but your insignificance saves you!

ISAAC (*Aside*): I'faith, then, my insignificance is the best friend I have. (*Aloud*): I'm going, dear Ferdinand. (*Aside*): What a curst hot-headed bully it is!

FROM # Lamp At Midnight

By BARRIE STAVIS

Barrie Stavis is a playwright who finds expression for his deep social and moral commitments in historical figures: the Bible's Joseph (in *Coat of Many Colors*), John Brown (in *Harper's Ferry*), Joe Hill (in *The Man Who Never Died*). In his most famous work, *Lamp at Midnight*, it is Galileo's struggle that provides Stavis with the dramatic confrontation that clothes his concern over matters of human conscience. The play contains many excellent choices for scene work. An actor and actress might especially like to use the scene between Galileo and Maria Celeste in Act III, Scene 5. The scene given here is from Act I, Scene 5. The characters are Galileo and Cardinal Bellarmin; the setting is an office in the Palace of the Inquisition.

BELLARMIN: No, Galileo, I offer you no hope. The Church cannot allow your new astronomy. Roman Catholicism is committed to the system of Aristotle.

GALILEO: But, Cardinal Bellarmin, all I ask is that the Church officially witness a scientific demonstration. In what way will that harm our Mother Church?

BELLARMIN: You still consider this a purely scientific question?

GALILEO: Is it not?

BELLARMIN: The scientific considerations are secondary.

GALILEO: How so, my Lord?

BELLARMIN: As Christianity developed, it became urgent to adopt a single official system of the universe. The Fathers of the Church found Aristotle's system most in accord with the spirit of Scripture. For hundreds of years the astronomy of Aristotle and the heavens of Christian theology have been as one! Now you come forward and say, "The old celestial hierarchy is false! I will introduce the true system!" (*Courteously*): And perhaps it is—for I respect your scientific work and think you personally a great man.

GALILEO: Thank you. And surely Your Eminence knows in what esteem I hold him?

BELLARMIN: But the truth or falsity of your system is not my concern! I must ask only one question: What will happen to Christian teaching if our system of the heavens were to be torn down and your system set up in its place? And the answer is: Christian truth would be destroyed!

GALILEO: My Lord!

BELLARMIN: You would transform the Church of the entire universe into the church of one insignificant clod of dirt, lost in space. . . .

GALILEO: My Lord!

BELLARMIN: You think I exaggerate? What will happen to the masses of men who have been nurtured in the belief that the world was created for man, and that he is God's especial concern? They would feel cheated, belittled, denigrated. They would turn in revulsion. Heresy, apostasy, atheism would be the order of the day. You would create a spiritual revolution.

GALILEO (*Stopping his ears with his hands—in deep agony*): Cardinal Bellarmin!

BELLARMIN (*Pulling GALILEO's hands away from his ears forcefully, in sharp contrast to his normally staid and venerable motions*): You can cry out my name—but do you think your voice imploring me to silence can change the significance of your discovery! Aristotle's heavens and the Christian heaven—the destruction of one would injure the other. This we cannot allow.

GALILEO (*Choked*): Oh, my Lord, you have just started a civil war inside me which will end in my destruction!

BELLARMIN (*Graciously*): No! No civil war and no destruction. Which do you hold more precious, your ephemeral science or your eternal Catholic soul?

GALILEO: Is *that* the choice?

BELLARMIN: What else?

GALILEO: No—that is not the choice. It will be to the eternal glory of the Church to be the first to acknowledge this concept. Think! Man by the power of his imagination and the reasoning of his intellect sweeping out beyond the farthest reaches of space and binding the universe into one noble law. Once able to comprehend this concept and hold it shining in his soul, man becomes a precious vessel.... Aristotle's system is false and mine is true!

BELLARMIN: My son, truth is a philosophic fiction! Make a declarative statement to me and I'll prove it to be lie or truth, whichever best suits the interest of our Holy Mother Church.

GALILEO: Your Eminence knows how highly I regard your theological learning.

BELLARMIN: Where the salvation of the soul is concerned, the Church teaches that there is no absolute truth. Something is true in proportion to the good or evil it does. For better or worse the Church fathers have committed us to Aristotle's astronomy. Were we to change now, the evil would be too great! Therefore there can be no change. (*With gracious comforting sympathy to* GALILEO): You've heard the admonition. You will obey and abandon your opinion?

GALILEO (*In a low choked voice*): I will obey.

FROM The Relapse

By SIR JOHN VANBRUGH

Give some actors a silk handkerchief and a snuffbox and they begin an effeminate, mincing sort of performance that to them signifies Restoration style. Such nonsense, of course, is neither Restoration nor stylish; it is simply misguided—and intolerable. The great plays of the Restoration have survived not because of their superficial frou-frou, but because beneath the chic there is sinew: shrewdly observed characters, biting satire, lusty humor, stinging wit.

The first objective of actors performing the following scene from Vanbrugh's *The Relapse*, then, is to try to create characters, not caricatures. The scene is from Act III, Scene 1, and comprises a confrontation between wealthy Lord Foppington and his impoverished younger brother, Young Fashion.

FASHION: Brother, your servant. How do you find yourself today?

FOPPINGTON: So well, that I have ardered my coach to the door. So there's no great danger of death this baut, Tam.

FASHION: I'm very glad of it.

FOPPINGTON (*Aside*): That I believe's a lie.
—Prithee, Tam, tell me one thing. Did nat your heart
cut a caper up to your mauth, when you heard I was
run through the bady?

FASHION: Why do you think it should?

FOPPINGTON: Because I remember mine did so,
when I heard my father was shat through the head.

FASHION: It then did very ill.

FOPPINGTON: Prithee, why so?

FASHION: Because he used you very well.

FOPPINGTON: Well? —naw strike me dumb, he
starved me. He has let me want a thausend women
for want of a thausend pound.

FASHION: Then he hindered you from making a
great many ill bargains, for I think no woman is
worth money, that will take money.

FOPPINGTON: If I were a younger brother, I should
think so too.

FASHION: Why, is it possible you can value a
woman that's to be bought?

FOPPINGTON: Prithee, why not as well as a padnag?

FASHION: Because a woman has a heart to dispose of; a horse has none.

FOPPINGTON: Look you, Tam, of all things that belang to a woman, I have an aversion to her heart; far when once a woman has given you her heart—you can never get rid of the rest of her bady.

FASHION: This is strange doctrine. But pray, in your amours how is it with your own heart?

FOPPINGTON: Why, my heart in my amours—is like my heart aut of my amours: *à la glace*. My bady, Tam, is a watch, and my heart is the pendulum to it; whilst the finger runs raund to every hour in the circle, that still beats the same time.

FASHION: Then you are seldom much in love?

FOPPINGTON: Never, stap my vitals.

FASHION: Why then did you make all this bustle about Amanda?

FOPPINGTON: Because she was a woman of an insolent virtue, and I thought myself piqued in honor to debauch her.

FASHION: Very well. (*Aside*): Here's a rare fellow for you, to have the spending of five thousand pounds a year. But now for my business with him. (*Aloud*): Brother, though I know to talk to you of business (especially of money) is a theme not quite so entertaining to you as that of the ladies, my necessities are such, I hope you'll have patience to hear me.

FOPPINGTON: The greatness of your necessities, Tam, is the worst argument in the world for your being patiently heard. I do believe you are going to make me a very good speech, but, strike me dumb, it has the worst beginning of any speech I have heard this twelvemonth.

FASHION: I'm very sorry you think so.

FOPPINGTON: I do believe thau art. But come, let's know thy affair quickly; far 'tis a new play, and I shall be so rumpled and squeezed with pressing through the crawd to get to my servant, the women will think I have lain all night in my clothes.

FASHION: Why then (that I may not be the author of so great a misfortune) my case in a word is this: the necessary expenses of my travels have so much exceeded the wretched income of my annuity that I have been forced to mortgage it for five hundred pounds, which is spent; so that unless you are so kind to assist me in redeeming it, I know no remedy but to go take a purse.

FOPPINGTON: Why, faith, Tam—to give you my sense of the thing, I do think taking a purse the best remedy in the world; for if you succeed, you are relieved that way; if you are taken—you are relieved t'other.

FASHION: I'm glad to see you are in so pleasant a humor; I hope I shall find the effects on't.

FOPPINGTON: Why, do you then really think it a reasonable thing I should give you five hundred paunds?

FASHION: I do not ask it as a due, brother; I am willing to receive it as a favor.

FOPPINGTON: Thau art willing to receive it anyhaw, strike me speechless. But these are damned times to give money in; taxes are so great, repairs so exorbitant, tenants such rogues, and periwigs so dear, that the devil take me, I am reduced to that extremity in my cash, I have been forced to retrench in that one article of sweet pawder, till I have braught it dawn to five guineas a manth. Naw judge, Tam, whether I can spare you five hundred paunds?

FASHION: If you can't, I must starve, that's all. (*Aside*): Damn him!

FOPPINGTON: All I can say is, you should have been a better husband.

FASHION: Oons, if you can't live upon five thousand a year, how do you think I should do't upon two hundred?

FOPPINGTON: Don't be in a passion, Tam, far passion is the most unbecoming thing in the world—to the face. Look you, I don't love to say anything to you to make you melancholy; but upon this occasion I must take leave to put you in mind that a running-horse does require more attendance than a coach-horse. Nature has made some difference 'twixt you and I.

FASHION: Yes, she has made you older. (*Aside*): Pox take her!

FOPPINGTON: That is nat all, Tam.

FASHION: Why, what is there else?

FOPPINGTON (*Looking first upon himself, then upon his brother*): Ask the ladies.

FASHION: Why, thou essence bottle, thou musk-cat, dost thou then think thou hast any advantage over me but what fortune has given thee?

FOPPINGTON: I do—stap my vitals.

FASHION: Now, by all that's great and powerful, thou art the prince of coxcombs.

FOPPINGTON: Sir—I am praud of being at the head of so prevailing a party.

FASHION: Will nothing then provoke thee? —Draw, coward!

FOPPINGTON: Look you, Tam, you know I have always taken you for a mighty dull fellow, and here is one of the foolishest plats broke out that I have seen a long time. Your paverty makes your life so burdensome to you, you would provoke me to a quarrel, in hopes either to slip through my lungs into my estate, or to get yourself run through the guts, to put an end to your pain. But I will disappoint you in both your designs; far with the temper of a philasapher, and the discretion of a statesman—I will go to the play with my sword in my scabbard. (*Exit* LORD FOPPINGTON.)

FROM **The Deputy**

By ROLF HOCHHUTH,
translated *By* RICHARD and
CLARA WINSTON

Like Barrie Stavis, whose work is represented earlier in this section, German playwright Rolf Hochhuth discusses urgent contemporary moral problems within a framework of historical events. *The Deputy*, because of its negative attitude toward the Pope's behavior during the Nazi regime, has aroused storms of hostility and controversy wherever it has been played. And Hochhuth concedes that there are many distortions of fact in his play. The central issue, however—the question of man's responsibility for his fellow man—is so important, according to the author, that it justifies such distortions.

The play offers many fine two-person scenes useful for two actors. The one given here is from Act I, Scene I. The setting is the reception room of the Papal Legation in Berlin. The time is August, 1942. The characters are the Papal Nuncio, sixty-nine years old, and Father Riccardo Fontana, a young priest.

NUNCIO: You weren't a bit nervous about coming
   to Berlin?
In Rome you were safe from bombs.
We have a raid every night.

RICCARDO: For someone of my age, Your Excellency,
a priest's life is much too safe.
My cousin was killed fighting in Africa.
I'm happy to have gotten out of Rome.

NUNCIO (*Amused*): How young you are! Twenty-
   seven
and Minutante already.
You will go far, young friend.
It was considered remarkable that His Holiness
became a Minutante at twenty-six.

RICCARDO: Your Excellency must consider
that I've chosen the right parent.

NUNCIO (*Cordially*): You are too modest.
If you were nothing but your father's son,
the Cardinal would never
have called you to the Secretariat of State.
(*Confidentially*): Is our Chief still
so ill disposed to me?

RICCARDO (*Embarrassed*): But, Your Excellency, no
   one is ill disp...

NUNCIO (*Placing a hand on his arm, then rising,
   holding the teacup*):
Come now, you too are well aware
that I have long been persona non grata in Rome...

RICCARDO (*Hesitantly, evasively*): Possibly at the
    Vatican
it seems easier to represent the Holy See
than here in Berlin. . . .

NUNCIO (*Vehemently justifying himself; he paces
    the room*):
The Pope should decide what he prefers:
peace with Hitler at any price, or else
let me be authorized to take a stand
the way my brother Nuncio in Slovakia
did two weeks ago when he spoke up
against the wholesale killing of Jews from Bratislava
in the Lublin district.
He made a strong protest . . .
My dear friend, what does Rome expect?
I would have resigned long ago
if I were not afraid my post would fall
into the hands of some nonentity!

RICCARDO: Does that mean Your Excellency favors
abrogating the Concordat with Hitler?

NUNCIO: Oh no, on the contrary. His late Holiness
    Pius XI
might well have done that.
But since the death of the old Pope
Herr Hitler has put a stop to certain measures
some of his more stupid underlings
wanted to take against us. He himself
is neutral in his official policy toward the Church,
impeccable, like Marshal Göring.
In Poland, though, he *is* trying to blackmail us.

Herr Goebbels, his Propaganda Minister,
can be talked to. You might almost call him
obliging. It's strange they haven't dared
touch Bishop Galen, even though he publicly
denounced, right from the pulpit,
the murder of the mentally ill.
Hitler actually gave in on that!

RICCARDO (*Enthusiastically*): Surely the Church can
    issue such demands,
Your Excellency! Especially now when bishops
in half of Europe are drumming up support
for Hitler's crusade against Moscow. On the train
I was reading what an army bishop
at the Eastern Front had said to...

NUNCIO (*Energetically, vexed*): You see, Father,
    that is precisely
what I oppose. We should *not*
be drumming up support for Hitler
as long as this wholesale killing
goes on behind his front lines. ...
London speaks
of seven hundred thousand Jews in Poland alone!
Of course, we've seen that sort of thing before.
Crusades begin with killing of the Jews.
But in such numbers—horrible.
I hardly think they are exaggerated.
You know how in Poland they are killing even the
    priests.
Our attitude should be one of great reserve.
For instance ... just recently, did the bishop
of Bohemia and Moravia *have* to plead with Herr
    Hitler

about that man Heydrich,
the Police Chief of Berlin and Prague ...

RICCARDO: The one who was shot, assassinated?

NUNCIO: Yes, right in the street. They took reprisals
against a whole village, including the women and
children.
Was it *necessary* for the Moravian bishop
to plead with Hitler hat in hand
if they might ring the bells for the deceased
and read a requiem for him?
(*With great indignation*):
A requiem for Heydrich is in bad taste.
That's really going too far....

FROM Death of a Salesman

By ARTHUR MILLER

Arthur Miller stands second only to Eugene O'Neill as an American dramatist capable of writing serious dramas that deal with the most significant theme available: the purgation and humanizing of man's soul. His most successful play, *Death of a Salesman*, has already assured itself the status: American classic. (Regrettably, there are few other plays that have achieved this. America has produced few giants of dramatic literature; Miller is one.)

In addition to the scene given here, two actors can study and profit by work on the Charley-Willy scene in Act I and the Willy-Howard scene (the "tape recorder" scene) in Act II. The opening scene of the play, for Willy and Linda, is a good choice for an actor and an actress. This scene comes immediately after that at the beginning of the play.

HAPPY (*With deep sentiment*): Funny, Biff, y'know? Us sleeping in here again? The old beds. (*He pats his bed affectionately.*) All the talk that went across those two beds, huh? Our whole lives.

BIFF: Yeah. Lotta dreams and plans.

HAPPY (*With a deep and masculine laugh*): About five hundred women would like to know what was said in this room.
(*They share a soft laugh.*)

BIFF: Remember that big Betsy something—what the hell was her name—over on Bushwick Avenue?

HAPPY (*Combing his hair*): With the collie dog!

BIFF: That's the one. I got you in there, remember?

HAPPY: Yeah, that was my first time—I think. Boy, there was a pig! (*They laugh, almost crudely.*) You taught me everything I know about women. Don't forget that.

BIFF: I bet you forgot how bashful you used to be. Especially with girls.

HAPPY: Oh, I still am, Biff.

BIFF: Oh, go on.

HAPPY: I just control it, that's all. I think I got less bashful and you got more so. What happened, Biff? Where's the old humor, the old confidence? (*He shakes BIFF's knee. BIFF gets up and moves restlessly about the room.*) What's the matter?

BIFF: Why does Dad mock me all the time?

HAPPY: He's not mocking you, he—

BIFF: Everything I say there's a twist of mockery on his face. I can't get near him.

HAPPY: He just wants you to make good, that's all. I wanted to talk to you about Dad for a long time, Biff. Something's—happening to him. He—talks to himself.

BIFF: I noticed that this morning. But he always mumbled.

HAPPY: But not so noticeable. It got so embarrassing I sent him to Florida. And you know something? Most of the time he's talking to you.

BIFF: What's he say about me?

HAPPY: I can't make it out.

BIFF: What's he say about me?

HAPPY: I think the fact that you're not settled, that you're still kind of up in the air . . .

BIFF: There's one or two things depressing him, Happy.

HAPPY: What do you mean?

BIFF: Never mind. Just don't lay it all to me.

Biff, do you really like the West?

HAPPY: But I think if you just got started—I mean—is there any future for you out there?

BIFF: I tell ya, Hap, I don't know what the future is. I don't know—what I'm supposed to want.

HAPPY: What do you mean?

BIFF: Well, I spent six or seven years after high school trying to work myself up. Shipping clerk, salesman, business of one kind or another. And it's a measly manner of existence. To get on that subway on the hot mornings in summer. To devote your whole life to keeping stock, or making phone calls, or selling or buying. To suffer fifty weeks of the year for the sake of a two-week vacation, when all you really desire is to be outdoors, with your shirt off. And always to have to get ahead of the next fella. And still—that's how you build a future.

HAPPY: Well, you really enjoy it on a farm? Are you content out there?

BIFF (*With rising agitation*): Hap, I've had twenty or thirty different kinds of jobs since I left home before the war, and it always turns out the same. I just realized it lately. In Nebraska when I herded cattle, and the Dakotas and Arizona, and now in Texas. It's why I came home now, I guess, because I realized it. This farm I work on, it's spring there now, see? And they've got about fifteen new colts. There's nothing more inspiring or—beautiful than the sight of a mare and a new colt. And it's cool there now, see? Texas is cool now, and it's spring. And whenever spring comes to where I am, I suddenly get the feeling, my God, I'm not gettin' anywhere! What the hell am I doing, playing around with horses, twenty-eight dollars a week! I'm thirty-four years old, I oughta be makin' my future. That's when I come running home. And now, I get here, and I don't know what to do with myself. (*After a pause*): I've always made a point of not wasting my life, and everytime I come back here I know that all I've done is to waste my life.

HAPPY: You're a poet, you know that, Biff? You're a—you're an idealist!

BIFF: No, I'm mixed up very bad. Maybe I oughta get married. Maybe I oughta get stuck into something. Maybe that's my trouble. I'm like a boy. I'm not married, I'm not in business, I just—I'm like a boy. Are you content, Hap? You're a success, aren't you? Are you content?

HAPPY: Hell, no!

BIFF: Why? You're making money, aren't you?

HAPPY (*Moving about with energy, expressiveness*): All I can do now is wait for the merchandise manager to die. And suppose I get to be merchandise manager? He's a good friend of mine, and he just built a terrific estate on Long Island. And he lived there about two months and sold it, and now he's building another one. He can't enjoy it once it's finished. And I know that's just what I would do. I don't know what the hell I'm workin' for. Sometimes I sit in my apartment—all alone. And I think of the rent I'm paying. And it's crazy. But then, it's what I always wanted. My own apartment, a car, and plenty of women. And still, goddammit, I'm lonely.

BIFF (*With enthusiasm*): Listen, why don't you come out West with me?

HAPPY: You and I, heh?

BIFF: Sure, maybe we could buy a ranch. Raise cattle, use our muscles. Men built like we are should be working out in the open.

HAPPY (*Avidly*): The Loman Brothers, heh?

BIFF (*With vast affection*): Sure, we'd be known all over the counties!

HAPPY (*Enthralled*): That's what I dream about, Biff. Sometimes I want to just rip my clothes off in the middle of the store and outbox that goddam merchandise manager. I mean I can outbox, outrun, and outlift anybody in that store, and I have to take orders from those common, petty sons-of-bitches till I can't stand it any more.

BIFF: I'm tellin' you, kid, if you were with me I'd be happy out there.

HAPPY (*Enthused*): See, Biff, everybody around me is so false that I'm constantly lowering my ideals...

BIFF: Baby, together we'd stand up for one another, we'd have someone to trust.

HAPPY: If I were around you—

BIFF: Hap, the trouble is we weren't brought up to grub for money. I don't know how to do it.

HAPPY: Neither can I!

BIFF: Then let's go!

HAPPY: The only thing is—what can you make out there?

BIFF: But look at your friend. Builds an estate and then hasn't the peace of mind to live in it.

HAPPY: Yeah, but when he walks into the store the waves part in front of him. That's fifty-two thousand dollars a year coming through the revolving door, and I got more in my pinky finger than he's got in his head.

BIFF: Yeah, but you just said—

HAPPY: I gotta show some of those pompous, self-important executives over there that Hap Loman can make the grade. I want to walk into the store the way he walks in. Then I'll go with you, Biff. We'll be together yet, I swear.

part 3

Scenes for
Two Women

FROM **The Autumn Garden**

By LILLIAN HELLMAN

As was noted in the introduction to another scene from this play given in Part One, Lillian Hellman's characters are an actor's delight. They are strongly motivated, highly individual, psychologically arresting. When they are intelligent, they are articulate; when they are stupid, they are touching in their inadequacy. They are never dull. They are always alive.

The two women in the scene below are among Miss Hellman's most subtle and interesting characterizations. Nina Denery is the sophisticated, attractive, and unhappy wife of a philandering painter. Sophie is a shrewdly realistic young French girl. This scene in Act III concerns the attitude of the women toward an episode of the night before, in which Nina's husband, Nick, stupidly compromised Sophie's reputation in the eyes of the Southern town in which the action passes, although in reality the incident was entirely innocent. (The incident itself makes another good acting exercise, as do many scenes in this strong play.)

SOPHIE: You are a pretty woman, Mrs. Denery, when your face is happy.

NINA: And you think my face is happy *this* morning?

SOPHIE: Oh, yes. You and Mr. Denery have had a nice reconciliation.

NINA (*Stares at her*): Er. Yes, I suppose so.

SOPHIE: I am glad for you. That is as it has been and will always be. (*She sits down.*) Now could I speak with you and Mr. Denery?

NINA (*Uncomfortably*): Sophie, if there was anything I can do— Er. Nick isn't here. I thought it best for us all—

SOPHIE (*Softly*): Ah. Ah, my aunt will be most sad.

NINA: Sophie, there's no good my telling you how sorry, how— What can I do?

SOPHIE: You can give me five thousand dollars, Mrs. Denery. American dollars, of course. (*Demurely; her accent from now on grows more pronounced.*) I have been subjected to the most degrading experience from which no young girl easily recovers. (*In French*): A most degrading experience from which no young girl easily recovers—

NINA (*Stares at her*): It sounds exactly the same in French.

SOPHIE: Somehow sex and money are simpler in French. Well. In English, then, I have lost or will lose my most beloved fiancé; I cannot return to school and the comrades with whom my life has been so happy; my aunt is uncomfortable and unhappy in the only life she knows and is now burdened with me for many years to come. I am utterly, utterly miserable, Mrs. Denery. I am ruined. (NINA *bursts out laughing.* SOPHIE *smiles.*) Please do not laugh at me.

NINA: I suppose I should be grateful to you for making a joke of it.

SOPHIE: You make a mistake. I am most serious.

NINA (*Stops laughing*): Are you? Sophie, it is an unpleasant and foolish incident and I don't wish to minimize it. But don't you feel you're adding considerable drama to it?

SOPHIE: No, ma'am. I did not say that is the way I thought of it. But that is the way it will be considered in this place, in this life. Little is made into very much here.

NINA: It's just the same in your country.

SOPHIE: No, Mrs. Denery. You mean it is the same in Brussels, or Strasbourg, or Paris, with those whom you would meet. In my class, in my town, it is not so. In a poor house if a man falls asleep drunk—and certainly it happens with us each Saturday night—he is not alone with an innocent young girl because the young girl, at my age, is not so innocent and because her family is in the same room, not having any other place to go. It arranges itself differently; you have more rooms and therefore more troubles.

NINA: Yes. I understand the lecture. (*Pauses.*) Why do you want five thousand dollars, Sophie?

SOPHIE: I wish to go home.

NINA (*Gently*): Then I will be happy to give it to you. Happier than you know to think we can do something.

SOPHIE: Yes. I am sure. But I will not accept it as largesse—to make you happy. We will call it a loan, come by through blackmail. One does not have to be grateful for blackmail money, nor think of oneself as a charity girl.

NINA (*After a second*): Blackmail money?

SOPHIE: Yes, ma'am. You will give me five thousand dollars because if you do not I will say that Mr. Denery seduced me last night. (NINA *stares at her, laughs.*) You are gay this morning, madame.

NINA (*Shocked*): Sophie, Sophie. What a child you are. It's not necessary to talk this way.

SOPHIE: I wish to prevent you from giving favors to me.

NINA: I intended no favors. And I don't like this kind of talk. Nick did not seduce you and I want no more jokes about it. (*Pleasantly*): Suppose we try to be friends—

SOPHIE: I am not joking, Mrs. Denery. And I do not wish to be friends.

NINA (*Gets up*): I would like to give you the money. And I will give it to you for that reason and no other.

SOPHIE: It does not matter to me what you would like. You will give it to me for my reason—or I will not take it.
(*Angrily*, NINA *goes toward door, goes into the room, then turns and smiles at* SOPHIE.)

NINA: You are serious? Just for a word, a way of calling something, you would hurt my husband and me?

SOPHIE: For me it is more than a way of calling something.

NINA: You're a tough little girl.

SOPHIE: Don't you think people often say other people are tough when they do not know how to cheat them?

NINA (*Angrily*): I was not trying to cheat you of anything—

SOPHIE: Yes, you were. You wish to be the kind

lady who most honorably stays to discharge—within reason—her obligations. And who goes off, as she has gone off many times, to make the reconciliation with her husband. How would you and Mr. Denery go on living without such incidents as me? I have been able to give you a second, or a twentieth, honeymoon.

NINA (*Angrily*): Is that speech made before you raise your price?

SOPHIE (*Smiles*): No. A blackmail bargain is still a bargain.

FROM Pride and Prejudice

dramatized *By* HELEN JEROME

Few actresses can resist a good strong confrontation with another character—particularly when the other character is also female. This scene is a good example of the genre. It is from Act III of Helen Jerome's dramatization of the Jane Austen novel. (It is assumed that *Pride and Prejudice* is well enough known so that no background needs filling in for this scene.)

Other good two-person scenes in this play, as one might suspect, are those between Elizabeth and Darcy.

LADY CATHERINE (*Seats herself, quite unperturbed*): Sit over there, Miss Bennet, where I can see you plainly.

(ELIZABETH *does so, amusedly.* LADY CATHERINE *eyes her an instant, reproof in her orbs.*)

ELIZABETH: I am feeling far from frivolous, I can assure you, ma'am.

LADY CATHERINE: Then you know why I am here?
(ELIZABETH *shakes her head, surprised.*) Has not
your conscience told you?

ELIZABETH (*Astounded*): My *conscience*?

LADY CATHERINE (*Angrily*): Miss Bennet, I am *not*
to be trifled with. I am celebrated for my frankness.
(*Fixes* ELIZABETH *with a gorgon glance.* ELIZABETH
stares at her wide-eyed.) Don't assume those innocent
airs.... *I'm* not a man! They will have no effect whatever on *me.* (ELIZABETH *raises her brows and waits
in silence.*) A report has reached me that you hope to
be married to my nephew, Mr. Darcy. (*Looks nar-
rowly at* ELIZABETH.) I would not insult him by asking about the truth of this... besides, he has left
Rosings... and I believe joined the Bingleys at
Netherfield. (*Looks suspiciously at* ELIZABETH, *who
just gives an impreceptible start of surprise.*) I have
come post haste from Rosings to let you know my
exact sentiments.

ELIZABETH (*Wonderingly*): What a long way to
come for such a purpose, Lady Catherine. Would not
a letter have been just as efficacious? (*Smiles.*) Especially as I know nothing of such a rumour.

LADY CATHERINE: Will you swear there is no
foundation for it?

ELIZABETH: Oh, no. I do not pretend to be as celebrated for frankness as your ladyship. So there are
certain questions I may not choose to answer... this
is one of them.

LADY CATHERINE: How—how *dare* you? I insist on knowing: has my nephew made you an offer of marriage?

ELIZABETH: But your ladyship has already declared that to be impossible.

LADY CATHERINE: It certainly *should* be. But your arts may have entangled him into forgetting what he owes to his family.

ELIZABETH (*Rising, going to her favorite place near the mantel, leaning against it, nonchalantly*): Then surely I should be the last to admit it. (*Laughs.*)

LADY CATHERINE (*Furiously*): Miss Bennet, do you know *who* I am? I have not been accustomed... (*Pauses, almost in a fit*): I am the nearest relative he has and entitled to know his dearest concerns.

ELIZABETH (*Calmly*): Then question *him.* You certainly are not entitled to know *mine.*

LADY CATHERINE: This marriage to which you have the effrontery to aspire ... will *never* take place. *Never!* Mr. Darcy is engaged to *my daughter.* (*Rises, stands hands on hips, facing* ELIZABETH.) Now what have you to say?

ELIZABETH: Only that if this is true, why are you worrying? How could he make an offer to me?... Or has he a case of bigamy in view? (*Smiles.*) It is still a crime in England, you know.

LADY CATHERINE (*Hesitatingly*): Well, they were intended for each other since infancy... my sister, the Lady Anne... hoped it with her last breath. (*Stands over* ELIZABETH *threateningly.*) Didn't you hear me say at Rosings, before the gentlemen came in after dinner, that I wish him to marry my daughter?

ELIZABETH (*Placidly*): Certainly. You gave expression to that wish several times. But if there were no *other* objections to my marriage with Mr. Darcy... your *wish* certainly would carry little weight.

LADY CATHERINE (*Threateningly*): Very well. If you persist. Don't expect to be received by his family... *or* his friends... *or*... *me*! Your name will never be mentioned by any of us! (*Nods several times to emphasize.*)

ELIZABETH: I must confess to your ladyship that this will not give me a moment's concern.

LADY CATHERINE (*Facing her with rage*): I am *ashamed* of you. Is *this* your gratitude for my hospitality?

ELIZABETH: Gratitude! But, Lady Catherine, I regard hospitality as a mutual grace, and by no means consider myself as an object for charity.

LADY CATHERINE (*Puffing about like a war horse*): Understand, my girl, I came here determined... I am not used to submitting to any person's whims nor brooking disappointments.

ELIZABETH (*Demurely*): That is unfortunate. It is rather late in life for your ladyship to be receiving your first taste of it....

LADY CATHERINE: Be silent. (*Storms up and down, then turns on* ELIZABETH.) The idea of you wanting to marry out of your own sphere!

ELIZABETH (*Smiling*): Oh, I should not consider it so. Mr. Darcy is a gentleman. I am the daughter of one.

LADY CATHERINE (*Coming close; with incredible vulgarity*): And pray what was your mother? A lady? (*Laughs scornfully.*) The daughter of a shopkeeper, with a brother...an *attorney!* You see, I am not deceived by your airs and graces. (ELIZABETH *looks at her silently.*)

ELIZABETH (*Thoughtfully*): And you, Lady Catherine, the daughter of a peer! It's strange how little birth seems to affect questions of taste...or gentleness of heart.

LADY CATHERINE: As if you could possibly know anything about such things. (*Brushing all that aside with a gesture*): Answer me once and for all, are you engaged to my nephew?

ELIZABETH: I must ask you to speak in a lower key...my sister is asleep out there (*indicates conservatory*). No, I am not engaged to anyone.

LADY CATHERINE (*Pleased, ready to be conciliatory*): And will you promise me you never will be?

ELIZABETH (*Quietly*): I will not.

LADY CATHERINE: Miss Bennet, I am shocked! (*Pauses, outraged, is about to rise, plumps down again.*) Then I refuse to leave until you have given me that promise.

ELIZABETH (*Rising, going to bell rope, pulls*): I hope your ladyship will have a pleasant journey back to Rosings. (*To the servant at the door*): Hill, her ladyship's coach, if you please.

The Women

By CLARE BOOTHE

No grouping of scenes exclusively for women would be complete without an extract from Clare Boothe's play for an all-female cast entitled, appropriately, *The Women*. Although it could hardly be said to be the definitive statement about the sex, the satire is certainly a hilariously biting comment on all-American bitchery; of the thirty-five characters, only four or five could be considered even partly sympathetic—and none of the four or five is overly bright!

Act 1, Scene 2, takes place in a beauty salon. Mary, an attractive young woman, married for several years, is having her nails done by Olga. Mary's friend Nancy has recommended Olga, and when Nancy leaves, Olga begins immediately talking about her as a logical way of drawing out this new customer.

OLGA: Funny, isn't she?

MARY: She's a darling.

OLGA (*Filing* MARY's *nails*): She's a writer? How

do those writers think up those plots? I guess the plot part's not so hard to think up as the end. I guess anybody's life'd make an interesting plot if it had an interesting end—Mrs. Fowler sent you in? (MARY, *absorbed in her book, nods.*) She's sent me three clients this week. Know Mrs. Herbert Parrish that was Mrs. Malcolm Leeds? Well, Mrs. Parrish was telling me herself about her divorce. Seems Mr. Parrish came home one night with lipstick on his undershirt. Said he always explained everything before. But *that* was something he just wasn't going to try to explain. Know Mrs. Potter? She's awful pregnant—

MARY (*She wants to read*): I know.

OLGA: Soak it, please. (*Puts* MARY's *hand in water. Begins on other hand.*) Know Mrs. Stephen Haines?

MARY: What? Why, yes, I—

OLGA: I guess Mrs. Fowler's told you about that! Mrs. Fowler feels awfully sorry for her.

MARY (*Laughing*): Oh, she does! Well, I don't. I—

OLGA: You would if you knew this girl.

MARY: What girl?

OLGA: This Crystal Allen.

MARY: Crystal Allen?

OLGA: Yes, you know. The girl who's living with

Mr. Haines. (MARY *starts violently*.) Don't you like
the file? Mrs. Potter says it sets her unborn child's
teeth on edge.

MARY (*Indignant*): Whoever told you such a
thing?

OLGA: Oh, I thought you knew. Didn't Mrs.
Fowler—?

MARY: No—

OLGA: Then you will be interested. You see, Crystal
Allen is a friend of mine. She's really a terrible man-
trap. Soak it, please. (MARY, *dazed, puts her hand in
the dish*.) She's behind the perfume counter at Saks'.
So was I before I got fi—left. That's how she met him.

MARY: Stephen Haines?

OLGA: Yeah. It was a couple of months ago. Us
girls wasn't busy. It was an awful rainy day, I remember. So this gentleman walks up to the counter. He
was the serious type, nice-looking, but kind of thin on
top. Well, Crystal nabs him. "I want some perfume,"
he says. "May I awsk what type of woman for?"
Crystal says, very Ritzy. That didn't mean a thing.
She was going to sell him Summer Rain, our feature
anyway. "Is she young?" Crystal says. "No," he says,
sort of embarrassed. "Is she the glamorous type?"
Crystal says. "No, thank God," he says. "Thank God?"
Crystal says and bats her eyes. She's got those eyes
which run up and down a man like a searchlight.
Well, she puts perfume on her palm and in the crook

of her arm for him to smell. So he got to smelling around and I guess he liked it. Because we heard him tell her his name, which one of the girls recognized from Cholly Knickerbocker's column— Gee, you're nervous. —Well, it was after that I left. I wouldn't of thought no more about it. But a couple of weeks ago I stopped by where Crystal lives to say hello. And the landlady says she'd moved to the kind of house where she could entertain her gentleman friend. "What gentleman friend?" I says. "Why, that Mr. Haines that she's had up in her room all hours of the night," the landlady says. —Did I hurt? (MARY *draws her hand away.*) One coat, or two? (*Picks up a red bottle.*)

MARY: None. (*Rises and goes to the chair where she has left her purse.*)

OLGA: But I thought that's what you came for? All Mrs. Fowler's friends—

MARY: I think I've gotten what all Mrs. Fowler's friends came for. (*Puts coin on the table.*)

OLGA (*Picks up coin*): Oh, thanks. —Well, goodbye. I'll tell her you were in, Mrs. —?

MARY: Mrs. Stephen Haines.

OLGA: Mrs. —? Oh, gee, gee! Gee, Mrs. Haines— I'm sorry! Oh, isn't there something I can do?

MARY: Stop telling that story!

OLGA: Oh, sure, sure, I will!

MARY: And please, don't tell anyone—(*Her voice breaks*)—that you told it to *me*—

OLGA: Oh, I won't, gee, I promise! Gee, that would be kind of humiliating for you! (*Defensively*): But in a way, Mrs. Haines, I'm kinda *glad* you know. Crystal is a terrible girl—I mean, she's terribly clever. And she's terribly pretty, Mrs. Haines—I mean, if I was you I wouldn't waste no time getting Mr. Haines away from her— (MARY *turns abruptly away*.) I mean, now you *know*, Mrs. Haines! (OLGA *eyes the coin in her hand distastefully, suddenly puts it down on the table and exits.* MARY, *alone, stares blankly in the mirror, then suddenly focusing on her image, leans forward, searching her face between her trembling hands.*)

FROM Uncle Vanya

By ANTON CHEKOV

In Chekov, the subtext is all. Consider the following scene: what we know about the characters comes mostly from what they do not say rather than from what they do say. Although superficially the women are communicating with one another, it might be more accurate to say that they are communicating with themselves in each other's presence.

Yelena and Sonya are about the same age, and yet they are worlds apart. Yelena is very beautiful, and is the wife of a pompous professor in his dotage. Sonya, the professor's daughter by his first marriage, is homely and a spinster. Both women are more than a little in love with Dr. Astrov. (See the Astrov-Yelena farewell from Act IV in Part One of this collection. The scene given here occurs toward the end of Act II.)

YELENA (*Opens the window*): The storm is over. What delicious air! (*A pause.*) Where is the doctor?

SONYA: He is gone. (*A pause.*)

YELENA: Sophie!

SONYA: What is it?

YELENA: How long are you going to be sulky with me? We have done each other no harm. Why should we be enemies? Let us make it up....

SONYA: I wanted to myself.... (*Embraces her.*) Don't let us be cross any more.

YELENA: That's right. (*Both are agitated.*)

SONYA: Has father gone to bed?

YELENA: No, he is sitting in the drawing room.... We don't speak to each other for weeks, and goodness knows why.... (*Seeing that the sideboard is open*): How is this?

SONYA: Mihail Lvovitch has been having some supper.

YELENA: And there is wine too.... Let us drink to our friendship.

SONYA: Yes, let us.

YELENA: Out of the same glass.... (*Fills it.*) It's better so. So now we are friends?

SONYA: Friends. (*They drink and kiss each other.*) I have been wanting to make it up for ever so long, but somehow I felt ashamed... (*Cries.*)

YELENA: Why are you crying?

SONYA: It's nothing.

YELENA: Come, there, there.... (*Weeps.*) I am a queer creature, I am crying too.... (*A pause.*) You are angry with me because you think I married your father from interested motives.... If that will make you believe me, I will swear it—I married him for love. I was attracted by him as a learned, celebrated man. It was not real love, it was all made up; but I fancied at the time that it was real. It's not my fault. And ever since our marriage you have been punishing me with your clever, suspicious eyes.

SONYA: Come, peace! peace! Let us forget.

YELENA: You mustn't look like that—it doesn't suit you. You must believe in everyone—there is no living if you don't. (*A pause.*)

SONYA: Tell me honestly, as a friend... are you happy?

YELENA: No.

SONYA: I knew that. One more question. Tell me frankly, wouldn't you have liked your husband to be young?

YELENA: What a child you are still! Of course I should! (*Laughs.*) Well, ask something else, ask away....

SONYA: Do you like the doctor?

YELENA: Yes, very much.

SONYA (*Laughs*): Do I look silly ... yes? He has gone away, but I still hear his voice and his footsteps, and when I look at the dark window I can see his face. Do let me tell you.... But I can't speak so loud; I feel ashamed. Come into my room, we can talk there. You must think me silly? Own up.... Tell me something about him.

YELENA: What am I to tell you?

SONYA: He is clever.... He understands everything, he can do anything.... He doctors people, and plants forests too....

YELENA: It is not a question of forests and medicine. ... My dear, you must understand he has a spark of genius! And you know what that means? Boldness, freedom of mind, width of outlook.... He plants a tree and is already seeing what will follow from it in a thousand years, already he has visions of the happiness of humanity. Such people are rare, one must love them.... He drinks, he is sometimes a little coarse—but what does that matter? A talented man cannot keep spotless in Russia. Only think what sort of life that doctor has! Impassable mud on the roads, frosts, snowstorms, the immense distances, the coarse savage peasants, poverty and disease all around him—it is hard for one who is working and struggling day after day in such surroundings to keep spotless and sober till he is forty. (*Kisses her.*) I wish you happiness with all my heart; you deserve it.... (*Gets up.*) But I am a tiresome, secondary character.... In music and in my husband's house, and in all the love affairs, everywhere in fact, I have always played a secondary part. As a matter of fact, if you come to think of it, Sonya, I am very, very unhappy! (*Walks up and down the stage in agitation.*) There is no happiness in this world for me, none! Why do you laugh?

SONYA (*Laughs, hiding her face*): I am so happy... so happy!

FROM The Vortex

By NOËL COWARD

Coward wrote *The Vortex* as a vehicle for himself; and when the play opened, with the author playing Nicky at the age of twenty-five, he became overnight the *enfant terrible* of the British theatre. A succession of gay, frivolous, and urbane comedies—with an occasional play of more serious pretensions—maintained Coward's position as *enfant terrible* for decades. ("Boys will be boys," says a character in Lillian Hellman's *The Autumn Garden*, "and in the South there is no age limit to boyishness." Thinking of Coward, one is tempted to add, "Nor in the British theatre!")

The best of Coward—*Private Lives, Hay Fever, Blithe Spirit*—remains popular to this day. Lesser Coward plays, however, also maintain a certain cachet today; for if they are no longer as daring and sophisticated as they seemed when they originally appeared, they at least have the purity of true period pieces. And there is always the special allure of Coward dialogue; no one else on earth could have written it.

This scene, from Act III, is for two women of middle age: the frivolous Florence, in desperate pursuit of youth, and her more sensible friend, Helen. (Two good scenes in Act II are those between Florence and her son, Nicky, and between Nicky and his fiancée, Bunty.)

(HELEN *is standing by the window of* FLORENCE'S *bedroom, gazing out at the moonlight.* FLORENCE *is obviously extremely hysterical.*)

HELEN: Florence, what *is* the use of going on like that?

FLORENCE: I wish I were dead!

HELEN: It's so cowardly to give way utterly—as you're doing.

FLORENCE: I don't care—I don't care!

HELEN: If you don't face things in this world, they only hit you much harder in the end.

FLORENCE: He loved me—he adored me!

HELEN: Never! He hadn't got it in him.

FLORENCE: After all I've done for him, to go to—to Bunty!

HELEN (*Leaving the window*): If it hadn't been Bunty it would have been someone else—don't you see how inevitable it was?

FLORENCE: How dared they! —Here! —In this house!

HELEN: That's a little thing; it doesn't matter at all.

FLORENCE: It does—it does—

HELEN: Florence, sit up and pull yourself together.

FLORENCE (*Sitting up slowly*): I think I'm going mad.

HELEN: Not a bit of it; you're just thoroughly hysterical.

FLORENCE: Give me some water.
(HELEN *goes to the bathroom and returns with a glass of water.*)

FLORENCE (*Taking it*): What time is it?

HELEN (*Looking at her watch*): Ten past one.

FLORENCE: Don't go to London by the early train, Helen; stay and come up with me in the car.

HELEN: Very well.

FLORENCE: Thank God, you were here!

HELEN: I wish I'd known what was happening; I might have done something.

FLORENCE: What can I do to get him back?

HELEN: Don't be silly.

FLORENCE: What can I do—what can I do?—

HELEN: Do you mean to say you'd *take* him back after to-night?

FLORENCE: No, never. Not if he crawled to me—never—

HELEN: Well, then, make up your mind definitely never to see him again whatever happens.

FLORENCE: Yes—I will.

HELEN: Why don't you go to bed now?

FLORENCE: I couldn't sleep.

HELEN: Put it all out of your mind—make an effort.

FLORENCE: I can't—I'm too unhappy.

HELEN: Think of Nicky.

FLORENCE: Nicky's young.

HELEN: That doesn't make it any better for him.

FLORENCE: He'll get over it in the long run.

HELEN: The long run never counts at the moment.

FLORENCE: He wasn't in love—really?

HELEN: As much as either you or he are capable of it.

FLORENCE: He's well rid of her. She'd never have appreciated him properly—she hasn't the intelligence.

HELEN: I don't agree with you there—she's got intelligence right enough.

FLORENCE: Treacherous little beast!

HELEN: Yes, but far-seeing.

FLORENCE: Are you standing up for her? Do you think it was *right* of her to get Tom away from me?

HELEN: Yes, quite right.

FLORENCE: Helen!

HELEN: To do her justice, she didn't deliberately set herself out to get him away from you at all. She discovered that in spite of the somewhat decadent years Tom was still her type, and likely to remain so. So with common sense she decided to shelve Nicky forthwith and go for him.

FLORENCE: Her type indeed!

HELEN: Yes, she'd have been quite a nice girl really if she'd been left alone and not allowed to go to Paris and get into the wrong set.

FLORENCE: You are extraordinary, Helen. Do you

realize that you're making excuses for the girl who's
betrayed your best friend?

HELEN: Don't be so utterly absurd. I'm not making
excuses, and, anyhow, she hasn't betrayed you. She
hardly knows you, in the first place, and she's just
followed her instincts regardless of anyone else's
feelings—as you've done thousands of times.

FLORENCE: Helen—you're being horrible to me!

HELEN: I'm not, I'm trying to make you see! You're
battering your head against silly cast-iron delusions,
and I want to dislodge them.

FLORENCE: Helen, I'm so unhappy—so desperately
unhappy.

HELEN: Yes, but not because you've lost Tom; it's
something far deeper than that.

FLORENCE: What then?

HELEN: You're on the wrong track, and have been
for years.

FLORENCE: I don't understand.

HELEN: You *won't* understand!
(FLORENCE *gets off the bed and goes over to the
dressing-table. She sits and stares at herself in the
glass for a moment without speaking.*)

FLORENCE: My eyes are sore. (*She powders her face and sprays a little scent on her hair.*) It's so lovely, this—and so refreshing.

HELEN: I think I'll go to bed now.

FLORENCE: No, wait a little longer with me—please, Helen—just a few minutes.

HELEN: It's so hot in here.

FLORENCE: Open the window then.

HELEN: All right. (*She goes to the window and opens it.*)
(FLORENCE *takes a cigarette out of a box and then shakes a scent-bottle and rubs the cigarette lightly with the stopper.*)

FLORENCE: Do you ever do this? It's divine.

HELEN: What a wonderfully clear night. You can see the hills right across the valley—the moon's quite strong.
(FLORENCE *goes to the window and stands next to* HELEN, *looking out—she is puffing her cigarette.*)

FLORENCE: I chose this room in the first place because the view was so lovely.

HELEN: Do you ever look at it?

FLORENCE (*Listlessly*): Of course I do, often!

HELEN: It's been raining. I wish you'd throw away that cigarette—it spoils the freshness.

FLORENCE (*Turning away*): It's soothing me—calming my nerves.

HELEN: I do wish I could help you—really!

FLORENCE: You are helping me, darling—you're being an angel.

HELEN (*Suddenly angry*): Don't talk so emptily, Florence; I'm worth more than that.

FLORENCE: I don't know what you mean.

HELEN: It sickens me to see you getting back so soon.

FLORENCE: Getting back?

HELEN: Yes, to your usual worthless attitude of mind.

FLORENCE: Helen!

HELEN: A little while ago you were really suffering for once, and in a way I was glad because it showed you were capable of a genuine emotion. Now you're glossing it over—swarming it down with your returning vanity; soon you won't be unhappy any more—just vindictive.

FLORENCE: Don't go on at me like that—I'm too wretched.

HELEN (*Going to her*): Florence, dear, forgive me, but it's true—and I don't want it to be.

FROM **Trifles**

By SUSAN GLASPELL

In the early part of this century, many serious American playwrights looked to the one-act play as a form worthy of their attention. The famous Provincetown Playhouse produced many of these, including a number by Eugene O'Neill. With the decline of interest in the one-act for professional use, most of these plays faded into oblivion. One of the few that have survived is *Trifles*, by Susan Glaspell. It is a subtle, moving play, in which a number of small details and low-key characterizations coalesce at the end with great force and impact.

The scene is a farm kitchen. The farmer has been murdered, his wife arrested for the killing. As the sheriff and his men search the upper floors of the house for clues, two neighbors, Mrs. Peters and Mrs. Hale, are straightening up the kitchen. (This is the second lengthy dialogue in the play between these women.)

MRS. HALE: She liked the bird. She was going to bury it in that pretty box.

MRS. PETERS (*In a whisper*): When I was a girl—my kitten—there was a boy took a hatchet, and before my eyes—and before I could get there—(*Covers her face an instant.*) If they hadn't held me back I would have— (*Catches herself, looks upstairs, falters weakly.*) —hurt him.

MRS. HALE (*With a slow look around her*): I wonder how it would seem never to have had any children around. (*Pause.*) No, Wright wouldn't like the bird—a thing that sang. She used to sing. He killed that, too.

MRS. PETERS (*Moving uneasily*): We don't know who killed the bird.

MRS. HALE: I knew John Wright.

MRS. PETERS: It was an awful thing was done in this house that night, Mrs. Hale. Killing a man while he slept, slipping a rope around his neck that choked the life out of him.

MRS. HALE: His neck. Choked the life out of him. (*Her hand goes out and rests on the birdcage.*)

MRS. PETERS (*With rising voice*): We don't know who killed him. We don't *know*.

MRS. HALE (*Her own feeling not interrupted*): If there'd been years and years of nothing, then a bird to sing to you, it would be awful—still, after the bird was still.

MRS. PETERS (*Something within her speaking*): I know what stillness is. When we homesteaded in Dakota, and my first baby died—after he was two years old, and me with no other then—

MRS. HALE (*Moving*): How soon do you suppose they'll be through looking for the evidence?

MRS. PETERS: I know what stillness is. (*Pulling herself back*): The law has got to punish crime, Mrs. Hale.

MRS. HALE (*Not as if answering that*): I wish you'd seen Minnie Foster when she wore a white dress with blue ribbons and stood up there in the choir and sang. (*A look around the room.*) Oh, I *wish* I'd come over here once in a while! That was a crime! That was a crime! Who's going to punish that?

MRS. PETERS (*Looking upstairs*): We mustn't—take on.

MRS. HALE: I might have known she needed help! I know how things can be—for women. I tell you, it's queer, Mrs. Peters. We live close together and we live far apart. We all go through the same things— it's all just a different kind of the same thing. (*Brushes her eyes, noticing the bottle of fruit, reaches out for it.*) If I was you, I wouldn't tell her her fruit was gone. Tell her it *ain't*. Tell her it's all right. Take this in to prove it to her. She—she may never know whether it was broke or not.

MRS. PETERS (*Takes the bottle, looks about for*

something to wrap it in; takes petticoat from pile of clothes, very nervously begins winding this around the bottle. In a false voice): My, it's a good thing the men couldn't hear us. Wouldn't they just laugh! Getting all stirred up over a little thing like a—dead canary. As if that could have anything to do with—with—wouldn't they *laugh!*

FROM Socrates Wounded

By ALFRED LEVINSON

The 1950's saw the blossoming of and coming-of-age of Off-Broadway and regional theater. Although many plays of distinction were written for this less financially and commercially oriented market, the greater majority of plays that appeared were virtually without merit. And even of the worthy minority, most achieved merit through theatrical daring rather than through literary and dramatic excellence. One of the exceptions was Alfred Levinson's Socrates Wounded, written in 1959. It is at once original, craftsmanlike, literate, insightful, and funny.

In this scene in Act II, Xanthippe, wife of Socrates, has just settled herself on a stool in front of her house and is eating her supper, when her friend Hera enters.

HERA (*Dry, sourish*): Eating on the terrace? Be lovely here in the twilight, except for the sewage gushing down the cobblestones.

XANTHIPPE: It's worse in there. (*Gestures backward.*) Stuffy—and hot air.

HERA: You mean your hero?

XANTHIPPE: That, too.

HERA: That's men for you. Can't breathe without bragging.

XANTHIPPE: So you've heard about it already.

HERA: Oh, Alcibiades' messengers have been splashing it all over Athens. "Great Victory." "Socrates a Hero." (*Pause.*) Just what did he do?

XANTHIPPE (*Anxiously*): What did you hear?

HERA: Something about his stopping a whole Persian line of battle.

XANTHIPPE (*Absorbed*): I could see him— I mean, I could see him stop a whole company with his questions. But not a line of battle. What could have happened?

HERA: Didn't he tell you anything?

XANTHIPPE: You know him, Hera. (HERA *nods: she knows him.*) Out in the streets he'll blabber to anyone he can catch—comes home and hardly a word.

HERA: That's the way they are.

XANTHIPPE: Any word from *your* husband?

HERA (*Grunts*): Uh-uh. He's still out there, what-ever it's called—I can't keep up with the names. Probably the last one demobilized. And he's a slow walker. Can't see *him* hurrying to get back—if he's alive.

XANTHIPPE (*Pats her arm*): Don't worry, dear. I'm sure he's fine.

HERA: Been through six battlefields already since we were married. Well, every time another war starts, I get some peace and quiet. He's just the opposite of your Socrates. At work, with the men, he's as meek as a lamb, keeps his mind on the metal. Comes home and chews my ear off. When do you think the next war will start?

XANTHIPPE: Let's hope never. (*Snorts.*) That Alci-biades. Soon as he spends what he steals out of this fight—or soon as he gets bored, whichever comes first—he'll show off his showmanship and his horse-manship and all his pretty uniforms.

HERA: What else has he got to do?

XANTHIPPE: And he's always prowling around here, visiting with Socrates. Zeus knows why.

HERA: He'll probably get Socrates a laurel crown. (*Slightly snide*): I'm sure he deserves it, whatever it is he did.

XANTHIPPE (*Mixed duty and pride in her defense*):
Of course. He deserves everything they'll give him.
Why—he's out all hours night and day thinking of
nothing but the good of Athens. Never his own wel-
fare. Or mine. He doesn't take any money from the
dandies. Not him. He's not a real teacher, says he.
Just heart and soul—worrying for all us Athenians.
(*A loud groan from inside.*) You hear? You hear that?
He's asleep now. Ever sleep with a thinker? Tossing,
turning, arguing with himself all night. Waking up at
two in the morning, all beady with sweat—even in
the winter, with one thin blanket. Mumbling about
"honor" and "virtue." I never have to worry about
my sinfulness, he's so wrapped up with what's inside
that dome of his. Sometimes he gets so restless, I
spend half the night on the floor.

HERA: I'd kick him out of bed fast—

XANTHIPPE: He doesn't budge—no matter how hard
I kick.

HERA (*After a pause, sighing wistfully*): My man's
a quiet sleeper—*too* quiet. (*Stretching and yawning*):
Well, it's getting dark. I'd better head home, clean
up. Though it isn't half as messy, without the men
around.

XANTHIPPE: It's such a comfort talking to you, Hera.
(*Looks toward* SOCRATES.) Listen to him snoring back
there. And all the muck of the battlefield still cover-
ing him—

HERA: Why don't you come over to my place? I wouldn't mind some company.

XANTHIPPE: You wouldn't? Isn't that nice. (*Crossing with her.*) It looks like it'll be a beautiful night, a big moon tonight— (*Hesitates.*) You think Socrates'll be all right? (*She stops.*)

HERA: What harm could come to him? Home in his own bed, safe—
(*Sounds of raucous cheering and shouting, offstage.*)

XANTHIPPE: Looks like the celebrating's started.

HERA (*Glumly*): They'll keep it up all night. Any excuse to get drunk. You coming?

XANTHIPPE (*Joining her*): I guess I can check in the morning, before I do my wash—see how he's doing—

HERA: He'll be there.
(*They go out.*)

FROM **The Chalk Garden**

By ENID BAGNOLD

Successful in both stage and screen versions, *The Chalk Garden* deals with the climate and nourishment necessary to growth—in both gardens and human spirits. Mrs. St. Maugham, a wealthy woman and frustrated gardener, has hired as governess to Laurel, her seemingly ungovernable granddaughter, a mysterious woman who calls herself Miss Madrigal and who offers no references. The air of suspicion surrounding Miss Madrigal grows murkier, and Laurel continually tries to unearth the older woman's secret. In Act II, during a water-color painting lesson, Laurel finally discovers that Miss Madrigal has been to a trial. The scene below follows this revelation.

Among several choice two-person scenes in this play are the Mrs. St. Maugham-Olivia scene at the end of Act I (Olivia is Laurel's mother) and the scene between Miss Madrigal and the man who was her judge, early in Act III.

LAUREL: So you've been to a trial?

MADRIGAL (*Crosses down stage to sofa*): I did not say I hadn't.

LAUREL (*Follows*): Why did you not say—when you know what store we both lay by it!

MADRIGAL (*Picks up two paintings from floor, puts them on small table*): It may be I think you lay too much store by it.

LAUREL (*Relaxing her tone and asking as though an ordinary light question*): How does one get in?

MADRIGAL: It's surprisingly easy. (*Sits on sofa, takes paint box.*)

LAUREL: Was it a trial for murder?

MADRIGAL (*Closing paint box*): It would have to be to satisfy you.

LAUREL: *Was* it a trial for murder? (*Sits above her on sofa.*)

MADRIGAL: Have you finished that flower?

LAUREL (*Rises; yawns*): As much as I can. I get tired of it. (*Pause.*) In my house—at home—there were so many things to do. (*She takes small table behind sofa and puts it right of armchair.*)

MADRIGAL: What was it like?

LAUREL: My home?

MADRIGAL: Yes.

LAUREL (*Doodling on a piece of paper and speaking as though caught unaware*): There was a stream. And a Chinese bridge. And yew trees cut like horses. And a bell on the weather-vane, and a little wood called mine—

MADRIGAL: Who called it that?

LAUREL (*Unwillingly moved*): She did—my mother. And when it was raining—we made an army of her cream pots and a battlefield of her dressing table— I used to thread her rings on safety pins—

MADRIGAL (*Picks up drawing book*): Tomorrow I will light that candle in the green glass candlestick and you can try to paint that.

LAUREL: What—paint the flame!

MADRIGAL: Yes.

LAUREL (*Doodling*): I'm tired of fire, too, Boss.

MADRIGAL (*As she notices* LAUREL *doodling*): Why do you sign your name a thousand times?

LAUREL: I am looking for which is me.

MADRIGAL (*Moves up stage on sofa*): Shall we read?

LAUREL (*Sits on desk chair*): Oh, I don't want to read.

MADRIGAL: Let's play a game.

LAUREL: All right. (*With meaning*): A guessing game.

MADRIGAL: Very well. Do you know one?

LAUREL: Maitland and I play one called "The Sky's the Limit."

MADRIGAL: How do you begin?

LAUREL (*Putting cushion from chair on floor and sitting down opposite her*): We ask three questions each but if you pass one I get a fourth.

MADRIGAL: What do we guess about?

LAUREL: Let's guess about each other. (*Full stop.*) We are both mysterious.

MADRIGAL (*Sententious*): The human heart *is* mysterious.

LAUREL: We don't know the first thing about each other, so there are so many things to ask.

MADRIGAL: But we mustn't go too fast. Or there will be nothing left to discover. Has it got to be the truth?

LAUREL: One can lie. But I get better and better at spotting lies. It's so dull playing with Maitland. He's so innocent. (MADRIGAL *folds her hands and waits.*) Now! First question— Are you a—*maiden* lady?

MADRIGAL (*After a moment's reflection*): I can't answer that.

LAUREL: Why?

MADRIGAL: Because you throw the emphasis so oddly.

LAUREL: Right. You don't answer. So now I get an extra question. Are you living under an assumed name?

MADRIGAL: No.

LAUREL: Careful! I'm getting my lie-detector working. Do you take things here at their face value?

MADRIGAL: No.

LAUREL: Splendid! You're getting the idea!

MADRIGAL (*Warningly*): This is to be your fourth question.

LAUREL (*Rising to centre, turns*): Yes. Yes. I must think—I must be careful. (*Shooting her question hard at* MADRIGAL): What is the full name of your married sister?

MADRIGAL (*Covers paint box with hands; staring a brief second at her*): Clarissa Dalrymple Westerham.

LAUREL: Is Dalrymple Westerham a double name?

MADRIGAL (*With ironical satisfaction*): You've *had* your questions.

LAUREL (*Gaily accepting defeat*): Yes, I have. Now yours. You've only three unless I pass one. (*Sits on cushion again.*)

MADRIGAL (*Pause*): Was your famous affair in Hyde Park on the night of your mother's marriage?

LAUREL (*Wary*): About that time.

MADRIGAL: What was the charge by the police?

LAUREL (*Wary*): The police didn't come into it.

MADRIGAL: Did someone follow you? And try to kiss you?

LAUREL (*Off her guard*): Kiss me! It was a case of Criminal Assault!

MADRIGAL (*Following that up*): How do you know— if there wasn't a charge by the police?

LAUREL (*Pausing a second; triumphant*): That's one too many questions! *Now* for the *deduction!* (*Cushion back on chair and sits.*)

MADRIGAL: You didn't tell me there was to be a deduction.

LAUREL: I forgot. It's the whole point. Mine's ready.

MADRIGAL: And what do you deduce?

LAUREL (*Taking breath*): —That you've changed so much you must have been something quite different. When you first came here you were like a rusty hinge that wanted oiling. You spoke to yourself out loud without knowing it. You had been *alone*. You may have been a missionary in Central Africa— You may have escaped from a private asylum— But as a maiden lady you are an impostor. (*Changing her tone slightly—slower and more penetrating*): About your assumed name I am not so sure. *But you have no married sister.*

MADRIGAL (*Lightly*): You take my breath away.

LAUREL (*Leaning back in chair; as lightly*): Good at it, aren't I?

MADRIGAL: Yes, for a mind under a cloud.

LAUREL: Now for your deduction!

MADRIGAL: Mine must keep. (*Rises with paint box, to down right door.*)

LAUREL: But it's the game! Where are you going?

MADRIGAL (*Pleasantly*): To my room. To make sure I have left no clues unlocked. (*Opens door.*)

LAUREL: To your past life?

MADRIGAL: Yes. You have given me so much warning. (*Exits down right.*)

FROM **The Ladies of the Corridor**

By DOROTHY PARKER and
ARNAUD D'USSEAU

One of the staples of the commercial theater
is the drama concerning several non-related
groups of people who are tied together by
similarity of problems or by sharing the
same physical locale. Such plays include
Grand Hotel, *Dinner At Eight*, and *The
Ladies of the Corridor*, from which a scene
is given here.

The common denominator for the several
groups of characters in this play is the hotel
in which they all live out their desperate
lives. Because of the various plots, the play
has many good scenes for student actors:
the Charles-Mrs. Nichols confrontation at
the end of Act II, Scene 3; the Mildred-
Harry scene, Act II, Scene 5; and three Paul-
Lulu scenes scattered through the play.

The scene given here opens Act II, Scene
4. It is the hotel apartment of middle-aged,
widowed Lulu Ames, who has been having
an affair with the younger Paul Osgood. At

the moment, Lulu is expecting Paul for dinner; she is slightly disappointed when her first caller proves to be her friend and confidante, Connie Mercer.

(*When the light comes up we discover* LULU *giving a last glance at the arrangements. She wears a charming teagown and looks her best. There is a knock on the corridor door.*)

LULU: Just a minute, darling!
(*She goes to the record player, puts on a record. Then she quickly goes to the table, lights the candles.*)

LULU: I won't be a second.
(*She gives the table a last quick look, touches a flower, then rushes to the door.* CONNIE *enters in street clothes and a hat.*)

CONNIE: Lulu, wait until I tell you!

LULU: Oh. Come in, Connie.

CONNIE: The most wonderful thing has happened! I'm a thousand miles up in the air. I'm jumping over little pink clouds.

LULU: Oh, really? What is it?

CONNIE: Well, that darling, dear, sweet, intelligent, humane boss of mine—

LULU: Just a minute, Con. (*She turns off the music, then goes and blows out the candles.*) Now tell me.

CONNIE: That blessed angel is sending me abroad. France and Italy and England. I'm going to buy furniture. I'm going to be gone for months with an expense account like a maharajah's.

LULU: Oh, that's lovely; perfectly lovely.

CONNIE: And do you know what else? When I come back I'm going to be a partner.

LULU: That's wonderful.

CONNIE: Sure it is, but I'll have to realize that later. I'm too excited about going to think about coming back. I honestly don't know what I'm doing. For heaven's sake, give me a drink to sober me up. (*She goes to the table.*) Do you and Paul have dinner here every night?

LULU (*Making a drink*): Not every night any more. He thinks it's wrong not to see something of other people.

CONNIE: Don't you see something of them too?

LULU: I tried. Honestly I did try. We went out three or four times with friends of his. But it all went wrong from the start. You see, these were people he knew when he was with Sally. I felt as if I was being compared.

CONNIE: Oh, Lulu, that imagination of yours!

LULU: That's what Paul said. He said it was silly.

Well, maybe it was, but that's the way I felt. And there's something else I keep feeling: he's enough for me; why aren't I enough for him?

CONNIE: Did you say that to him?

LULU: Yes, I'm afraid I've said it to him a lot of times. He didn't like it. Connie, I didn't think it could happen, but I've been making scenes. I always thought people who made scenes were disgusting. I still do. (*She goes to the window, looks down into the street.*)

CONNIE: Ah, Lulu, get hold of yourself.

LULU: Don't you think I've tried? (*She moves away from the window.*) Connie, I'm a pig; a filthy, self-centered pig. Here you are with your wonderful news, and I go spoiling your pleasure with my stupid tales of woe.

CONNIE: Please, Lulu. I'm all set. Now what we've got to do is get you fixed up.

LULU: I don't know how to get myself fixed up. There's something lacking. I guess there's something lacking in a lot of women; nobody's ever one of a kind. We were told you grew up, you got married, and there you were. And so we did, and so there we were. But our husbands, they were busy. We weren't part of their lives; and as we got older we weren't part of anybody's lives, and yet we never learned how to be alone. It's different with girls now. But that's the way it was with me.... Connie, do you really think it matters that a woman is older than a man?

CONNIE: Only if they think about it.

LULU: Paul doesn't think about it. I'm the one who does.

CONNIE: Then stop.

LULU: Nasty little thing. He's late again.

CONNIE: Lulu, you've got to get out of this.

LULU: I tried. (*She indicates the books on the coffee table.*) I took a big adventurous trip to the lending library. Oh, not Paul's. I didn't dare go to the one in his shop. He says the lending-library book is the badge of the unwanted woman. But I can't read, even mysteries. A beautiful young girl gets chopped into little pieces with an ax, and all I think is: And she thinks she's got trouble! No; more and more I just sit here and play my game.

CONNIE: What game?

LULU: I make believe Paul and I are going to be married. I even decided what I would wear. I had a hard time choosing between beige and gray, but I think definitely gray. Not old-lady gray, you know. Sort of pinkish gray. And I think those little butterfly orchids. I love yellow and gray, don't you? Do you think I'm crazy?

CONNIE: Not quite.

LULU: Well, then, I'll show you I really am. Wait a

second. (*She goes quickly into the bedroom.* CONNIE *looks after her, troubled.* LULU *returns with a charming little gray hat with a veil floating from it.*) I saw exactly the right wedding hat, so I bought it.

CONNIE: Yes, it's darling. Lulu, why don't you come abroad with me?

LULU: No, Con. It's sweet of you, but I can't.

CONNIE: Sure you can. And don't think you'll be left alone. Look, I'll have time off. I'll take time off. Come on.

LULU: No, I've got to stay here. (*In a sudden outburst*): Where on earth is he? Why does he have to be so late? If people want to see people, they come when they say they will!

CONNIE: Easy, Lulu, easy.

LULU (*Sobbing*): Oh, Connie, why did it have to happen to me so late? I can't lose it! I can't lose it!

FROM Separate Tables

By TERENCE RATTIGAN

Like *The Ladies of the Corridor*, this play by Rattigan concerns several groups of people whose lives are bound by their residence in a hotel. Actually, *Separate Tables* comprises two long one-act plays: "Table by the Window" and "Table Number Seven," from which this scene is taken.

Miss Cooper is the warm and sensible manageress of the hotel; Sibyl is the repressed, dowdy, late-thirtyish daughter of a domineering mother. Sibyl has been friendly with another guest, one Major Pollack; but the Major has now been exposed as a fraud, who has been found guilty of annoying women in darkened movie theaters.

Both one-acts that comprise *Separate Tables* have several strong two-person scenes; the one between Sibyl and the Major which immediately precedes the scene given here is especially effective.

MISS COOPER: Your mother's gone up to dress for dinner, Miss Railton-Bell. She told me I'd find you in the writing room lying down and I was to tell you that you can have your meal upstairs tonight, if you'd rather.

SIBYL: That's all right.

MISS COOPER (*Sympathetically*): How are you feeling now?

SIBYL (*Brusquely*): All right.

MISS COOPER (*Quietly*): Is there anything I can do to help you?

SIBYL (*With her back to* MISS COOPER; *angrily*): No. Nothing. And please don't say things like that. You'll make me feel bad again, and I'll make a fool of myself. I feel well now. He's going, and that's good. I despise him.

MISS COOPER: Do you? I wonder if you should?

SIBYL (*Over her shoulder*): He's a vile, wicked man, and he's done a horrible, beastly thing. It's not the first time, either. He admits that.

MISS COOPER: I didn't think it was.

SIBYL (*Looking out of the window*): And yet you told him he could stay on in the hotel if he wanted to? That's wicked, too.

MISS COOPER (*Moving to* SIBYL): Then I suppose I *am* wicked, too. (*She puts her hand on* SIBYL'S *arm.*) Sibyl, dear . . .

SIBYL: Why is everyone calling me Sibyl this evening? Please stop. You'll only make me cry.

MISS COOPER: I don't mean to do that. I just mean to help you. (SIBYL *breaks down suddenly, but now quietly and without hysteria.* MISS COOPER *puts an arm around* SIBYL.) That's better. Much better.

SIBYL: It's so horrible.

MISS COOPER: I know it is. I'm very sorry for you.

SIBYL: He says we're alike—he and I.

MISS COOPER: Does he?

SIBYL: He says we're both scared of life and people and sex. There—I've said the word. He says I hate *saying* it even, and he's right. I do. What's the matter with me? There must be something the matter with me.

MISS COOPER: Nothing very much, I should say. Shall we sit down?

(*She gently propels* SIBYL *to the sofa.* SIBYL *sits on the sofa at the left side.* MISS COOPER *sits upstage of* SIBYL.)

SIBYL: I'm a freak, aren't I?

MISS COOPER (*In matter-of-fact tones*): I never know what that word means. If you mean you're different from other people, then, I suppose, you are a freak. But all human beings are a bit different from each other, aren't they? What a dull world it would be if they weren't.

SIBYL: I'd like to be ordinary.

MISS COOPER: I wouldn't know about that, dear. You see, I've never met an ordinary person. To me all people are extraordinary. I meet all sorts here, you know, in my job, and the one thing I've learnt in five years is that the word normal, applied to any human being, is utterly meaningless. In a sort of way, it's an insult to our Maker, don't you think, to suppose that He could possibly work to any set pattern?

SIBYL: I don't think Mummy would agree with you.

MISS COOPER: I'm fairly sure she wouldn't. Tell me—when did your father die?

SIBYL: When I was seven.

MISS COOPER: Did you go to school?

SIBYL: No. Mummy said I was too delicate. I had a governess some of the time, but most of the time Mummy taught me herself.

MISS COOPER: Yes. I see. And you've never really been away from her, have you?

SIBYL: Only when I had a job, for a bit. (*Proudly*): I was a salesgirl in a big shop in London—Jones &

Jones. I sold lampshades. But I got ill, though, and had to leave.

Miss Cooper (*Brightly*): What bad luck! Well, you must try again some day, mustn't you?

Sibyl: Mummy says no.

Miss Cooper: Mummy says no. Well then, you must just try to get Mummy to say yes, don't you think?

Sibyl: I don't know how.

Miss Cooper: I'll tell you how. By running off and getting a job on your own. She'll say yes quick enough then. (*She pats* Sibyl's *knee affectionately and rises.*) I have my menus to do.

Sibyl (*Urgently*): Will he be all right, do you think?

Miss Cooper: The Major? I don't know. I hope so.

Sibyl: In spite of what he's done, I don't want anything bad to happen to him. I want him to be happy. Is it a nice hotel—this one in West Kensington?

Miss Cooper: Very nice.

Sibyl: Do you think he'll find a friend there? He told me just now that he'd always be grateful to me for making him forget how frightened he was of people.

MISS COOPER: He's helped you, too, hasn't he?

SIBYL: Yes.

MISS COOPER (*After a pause*): I hope he'll find a friend in the new hotel.

SIBYL: So do I. Oh, God, so do I!

FROM **Autumn Crocus**

By C. L. ANTHONY

A gentle and touching play, *Autumn Crocus* is the story of an English spinster, Fanny, traveling in Europe on holiday with a slightly older friend, Edith. Fanny falls in love with Steiner, a handsome innkeeper, who proves to be married. Fanny knows that she must forget him, and continue on her travels with Edith; and yet. . . .

Act II, Scene 2, comprises a long dialogue between Fanny and Steiner. This scene is from the opening of Act III.

EDITH: Fanny dear, do pull yourself together and get ready.

FANNY: I'm not going.

EDITH: Not going?

FANNY: No.

EDITH: You really are too trying, Fanny. We went over all this last night. You know we can't stay.

FANNY: You can't. But I can—alone.

EDITH: Fanny!

FANNY: I'm sorry, Edith.

EDITH: I should think you were—springing this on me at the last minute. You know I can't possibly leave you alone—and the bus'll be here in a few minutes.

FANNY: Well, I can't go by that bus, anyhow—I haven't packed.

EDITH: I've packed for you.

FANNY: Thank you. That was nice of you. But I'm not going. I've made up my mind. This is what I've been waiting for all my life.

EDITH: What is?

FANNY: The place—the mountains—everything.

EDITH: Fanny, I think you've gone stark, staring mad. You've never taken all this interest in mountains before.

FANNY: I've always liked mountains.

EDITH: But not to the extent of ruining our holiday— to say nothing of poor old Travers waiting for us in Venice. If it wasn't for her I'd give in to you—but as it is—

FANNY: But I don't want you to give in. I want you to join Travers.

EDITH: Thank you very much—but if I'd wanted to spend a holiday alone with Travers I could have done it before now. And what on earth can you do here by yourself?

FANNY: Walk and climb.

EDITH: You can't alone—it's dangerous.

FANNY: Not very. Besides, I daresay someone would go with me.

EDITH: But there's no one here for you to be friendly with—and you know how miserable you are if you're alone.

FANNY: I shan't be miserable.

EDITH: Well, I shall, shut up in Venice with Travers. I can't think what's happened to you, Fanny; you're not usually selfish like this.

FANNY: I don't mean to be selfish, Edith. It's something important to me—I *must* stay. (*She rises and walks to the windows.*)

EDITH: *Must* stay! (*Sees shawl which* FANNY *carries over her arm.*) What on earth's that?

FANNY: Just a shawl—Herr Steiner lent it to me because it was cold in the early morning on the mountains.

EDITH: Herr Steiner? The innkeeper? Was he on the mountains, too?

FANNY: Yes—for a little while.

EDITH: Did you go out with him?

FANNY: No—I just met him.

EDITH: By accident?

FANNY: Yes—at least, not exactly. He knew I was going.

EDITH: How did he know?

FANNY (*Utterly unable to withstand* EDITH's *hammer-like questions*): He—he suggested it last night.

EDITH: Why didn't you tell me?

FANNY: I left you a note—I couldn't tell you—you were nearly asleep.

EDITH: Asleep! Fanny, were you talking to that man on the balcony last night? —I thought I heard voices, but I was too sleepy to be sure. Were you, Fanny? (FANNY *does not reply*.) Were you?

FANNY: Only for a few minutes—he came out on

the next balcony. (*She is beginning to show signs of distress.*)

EDITH: And you arranged to meet him on the mountains?

FANNY: No, I didn't; he just suggested that I should go out on them—

EDITH: And then came to meet you with his wife's shawl!

FANNY: It isn't his wife's!

EDITH: Fanny! Fanny! Is this the reason that you want to stay—because of this man?

FANNY: No—no—don't cross-examine me in this way—you've no right—

EDITH: I have a right. I think you must have gone mad—talking to this man in your dressing-gown—running about the mountains with a common innkeeper—

FANNY: He's not common! And, anyway, he's got nothing to do with it. I'm staying here because of the place.

EDITH: Fanny, don't try to bluff me—you're no good at it. You've got to tell me the truth. Did he persuade you to stay?

FANNY: No—I tell you he's got nothing to do with it. (*She is getting more and more worked up.*) Don't keep questioning me, Edith—leave me alone!

EDITH: Fanny! Has he been making love to you?

FANNY: No! No! It's no use your going on—I won't answer your questions.

EDITH: You are answering my questions. Do you think I can't read the whole thing in your face?

FANNY (*Overcome, sinks down at the table and sobs; incoherently*): Don't! Don't look at me—it's nothing to do with you—leave me alone! You're hateful—cruel—

EDITH (*Making a great effort to control her horror and emotion*): Fanny, I don't mean to be cruel—it's just that I'm so appalled. Look, dear, pull yourself together. Let me try to help you. Tell me about it—I'll do my best to understand. (*As FANNY still sobs*): You—you've fallen in love with him—that's it, isn't it?

FANNY (*Through her tears, almost inaudible*): Yes.

EDITH: And does he know?

FANNY: Yes.

EDITH: And does he pretend to be in love with you?

FANNY: It isn't pretence.

EDITH: Oh, well, perhaps he thinks he is—you're very pretty sometimes. What does he want you to do?

FANNY (*Her sobs have ceased, and she answers* EDITH's *questions quietly and miserably*): Just to stay here with him.

EDITH: Do you know what that means?

FANNY: Yes, Edith.

EDITH: You can't be—just friends with a man of his type.

FANNY: I don't want to be just friends.

EDITH: Oh, it's so horrible—to think of you, of all people! I—I don't know what to say to you.

FANNY: Then don't say anything.

EDITH: But I must. This may ruin your life. Have you thought what it means? You can never come back to the school.

FANNY: Why not?

EDITH: Miss Hill would never keep you.

FANNY: You mean you'd tell?

EDITH: No, of course not. But you'd be different—you'd even look different—

FANNY: I'd only look happy.

EDITH: You couldn't look happy with a sordid thing like that in your mind.

FANNY: It's not sordid!

EDITH: But it is! Have you thought of the scandal here?

FANNY: No one will know.

EDITH: Everyone will know. You can't hide anything. You'll just walk about looking happy—as you call it. And how about Frau Steiner—have you thought of her?

FANNY: Yes, I've been thinking about her all the morning. But she won't know—she shan't—we'll hide it somehow. It isn't as if I wanted to take him from her altogether. And, anyhow, I can't help it; it may be wicked, but it's happened. And it doesn't feel wicked to me.

EDITH: It *is* wicked—to her and to yourself. Oh, I can't think of it—a girl of your type and a man of his! Oh, I know he's unusual—charming even—but you're not the same class—

FANNY: What is my class? The daughter of a poor clergyman! His people have been here for hundreds of years.

EDITH: It doesn't make any difference—he's a peasant. (*Brokenly*): Fanny, hasn't our friendship meant anything to you? I'm fonder of you than anyone in the world, and if this happens I shall never be able to look at you again. It isn't that I'm narrow-minded, but it's—just unthinkable for you. Heaven knows, if it were a happy marriage I'd be glad for you, but this—!

FANNY: Don't, Edith! Please! Oh, I don't want to be ungrateful to you—to hurt you—but this—can't you see it's beautiful to me? You're making it ugly, sordid—

EDITH: It *is* sordid—not what's in your mind, but what it entails. It may be a romance to you both now, but how do you imagine he'll think of you afterwards? Just as a light woman—

FANNY: No!

EDITH: Why not? It'll be true.

Copies of this play, individual paper covered acting editions, are available from Samuel French, Inc., 25 West 45th Street, New York, New York or 7623 Sunset Boulevard, Hollywood, California, or in Canada Samuel French, (Canada) Ltd., 26 Grenville Street, Toronto, Canada.

FROM Romeo and Juliet

By WILLIAM SHAKESPEARE

This scene is probably the most conspicuous exception to the stricture mentioned in the Introduction to this book that a scene had to be fairly unfamiliar to students to earn a place in this collection. It is, however, simply too good a scene to omit.

Act III, Scene 2 begins with Juliet's soliloquy, "Gallop apace, you fiery-footed steeds...." The lines below come at the end of that beautiful speech.

JULIET: O, here comes my nurse,
And she brings news; and every tongue that speaks
But Romeo's name speaks heavenly eloquence.

(NURSE *enters with cords.*)

JULIET: Now, nurse, what news? What hast thou
   there? the cords
That Romeo bid thee fetch?

NURSE (*Throwing them down*): Ay, ay, the cords.

JULIET: Ay me! what news? why dost thou wring thy
    hands?

NURSE: Ay, well-a-day! he's dead, he's dead, he's
    dead!
We are undone, lady, we are undone!
Alack the day! he's gone, he's kill'd, he's dead!

JULIET: Can heaven be so envious?

NURSE: Romeo can,
Though heaven cannot: O Romeo, Romeo!
Who ever would have thought it? Romeo!

JULIET: What devil art thou, that dost torment me
    thus?
This torture should be roar'd in dismal hell.
Hath Romeo slain himself? say thou but 'I,'
And that bare vowel 'I' shall poison more
Than the death-darting eye of cockatrice:
I am not I, if there be such an I;
Or those eyes shut, that make thee answer 'I.'
If he be slain, say 'I'; or if not, no:
Brief sounds determine of my weal or woe.

NURSE: I saw the wound, I saw it with mine eyes,—
God save the mark!—here on his manly breast:
A piteous corse, a bloody piteous corse;
Pale, pale as ashes, all bedaub'd in blood,
All in gore-blood: I swounded at the sight.

JULIET: O, break, my heart! poor bankrupt, break at
    once!

To prison, eyes, ne'er look on liberty!
Vile earth, to earth resign; end motion here;
And thou and Romeo press one heavy bier!

NURSE: O Tybalt! Tybalt, the best friend I had!
O courteous Tybalt! honest gentleman!
That ever I should live to see thee dead!

JULIET: What storm is this that blows so contrary?
Is Romeo slaughter'd, and is Tybalt dead?
My dear-loved cousin, and my dearer lord?
Then, dreadful trumpet, sound the general doom!
For who is living, if those two are gone?

NURSE: Tybalt is gone, and Romeo banished;
Romeo that kill'd him, he is banished.

JULIET: O God! did Romeo's hand shed Tybalt's
    blood?

NURSE: It did, it did; alas the day, it did!

JULIET: O serpent heart, hid with a flowering face!
Did ever dragon keep so fair a cave?
Beautiful tyrant! fiend angelical!
Dove-feather'd raven! wolvish-ravening lamb!
Despised substance of divinest show!
Just opposite to what thou justly seem'st,
A damned saint, an honourable villain!
O nature, what hadst thou to do in hell,
When thou didst bower the spirit of a fiend
In mortal paradise of such sweet flesh?
Was ever book containing such vile matter

So fairly bound? O, that deceit should dwell
In such a gorgeous palace!

NURSE: There's no trust,
No faith, no honesty in men; all perjured,
All forsworn, all naught, all dissemblers.
Ah, where's my man? give me some aqua vitae:
These griefs, these woes, these sorrows make me old.
Shame come to Romeo!

JULIET: Blister'd be thy tongue
For such a wish! he was not born to shame:
Upon his brow shame is ashamed to sit;
For 'tis a throne where honour may be crown'd
Sole monarch of the universal earth.
O, what a beast was I to chide at him!

NURSE: Will you speak well of him that kill'd your
cousin?

JULIET: Shall I speak ill of him that is my husband?
Ah, poor my lord, what tongue shall smooth thy name,
When I, thy three-hours wife, have mangled it?
But, wherefore, villain, didst thou kill my cousin?
That villain cousin would have kill'd my husband:
Back, foolish tears, back to your native spring;
Your tributary drops belong to woe,
Which you, mistaking, offer up to joy.
My husband lives, that Tybalt would have slain;
And Tybalt's dead, that would have slain my husband:
All this is comfort; wherefore weep I then?
Some word there was, worser than Tybalt's death,
That murder'd me: I would forget it fain;

But, O, it presses to my memory,
Like damned guilty deeds to sinners' minds:
'Tybalt is dead, and Romeo—banished;'
That 'banished,' that one word 'banished,'
Hath slain ten thousand Tybalts. Tybalt's death
Was woe enough, if it had ended there:
Or, if sour woe delights in fellowship
And needly will be rank'd with other griefs,
Why follow'd not, when she said 'Tybalt's dead,'
Thy father, or thy mother, nay, or both,
Which modern lamentation might have moved?
But with a rearward following Tybalt's death,
'Romeo is banished,' to speak that word,
Is father, mother, Tybalt, Romeo, Juliet,
All slain, all dead. 'Romeo is banished!'
There is no end, no limit, measure, bound,
In that word's death; no words can that woe sound.
Where is my father, and my mother, nurse?

NURSE: Weeping and wailing over Tybalt's corse:
Will you go to them? I will bring you thither.

JULIET: Wash they his wounds with tears: mine
      shall be spent
When theirs are dry, for Romeo's banishment.
Take up those cords: poor ropes, you are beguiled,
Both you and I; for Romeo is exiled:
He made you for a highway to my bed;
But I, a maid, die maiden-widowed.
Come, cords, come, nurse; I'll to my wedding-bed;
And death, not Romeo, take my maidenhead!

NURSE: Hie to your chamber: I'll find Romeo
To comfort you: I wot well where he is.

Hark ye, your Romeo will be here at night:
I'll to him; he is hid at Laurence' cell.

JULIET: O, find him! give this ring to my true knight,
And bid him come to take his last farewell.

FROM Mary of Scotland

By MAXWELL ANDERSON

Verse drama has not been able to put down roots in American soil. There have been many explanations offered for this, but none has proved truly satisfactory; and with the continuing breaking-up of traditional theatrical forms, we may yet see a body of native American plays in verse.

Maxwell Anderson alone was a successful American playwright writing poetic drama. *Winterset, High Tor, Elizabeth the Queen,* and *Mary of Scotland* have all reached wide audiences and an enduring place in dramatic literature.

This scene is the second half of the final confrontation between the two queens that ends *Mary of Scotland.* The action passes in a cell-like room at Carlisle Castle, where Mary is Elizabeth's prisoner.

MARY: Elizabeth—I have been here a long while
Already—it seems so. If it's your policy
To keep me—shut me up—. I can argue no more—

No—I beg now. There's one I love in the north,
You know that—and my life's there, my throne's there,
    my name
To be defended—and I must lie here darkened
From news and from the sun—lie here impaled
On a brain's agony—wondering even sometimes
If I were what they said me—a carrion-thing
In my desires—can you understand this?—I speak it
Too brokenly to be understood, but I beg you
As you are a woman and I am—and our brightness
    falls
Soon enough at best—let me go, let me have my life
Once more—and my dear health of mind again—
For I rot away here in my mind—in what
I think of myself—some death-tinge falls over one
In prisons—

   ELIZABETH: It will grow worse, not better. I've
    known
Strong men shut up alone for years—it's not
Their hair turns white only; they sicken within
And scourge themselves. If you would think like a
    queen
This is no place for you. The brain taints here
Till all desires are alike. Be advised and sign
The abdication.

   MARY: Stay now a moment. I begin to glimpse
Behind this basilisk mask of yours. It was this
You've wanted from the first.

   ELIZABETH: This that I wanted?

   MARY: It was you sent Lord Throgmorton long ago

When first I'd have married Bothwell. All this while
Some evil's touched my life at every turn.
To cripple what I'd do. And now—why now—
Looking on you—I see it incarnate before me—
It was your hand that touched me. Reaching out
In little ways—here a word, there an action—this
Was what you wanted. I thought perhaps a star—
Wildly I thought it—perhaps a star might ride
Astray—or a crone that burned an image down
In wax—filling the air with curses on me
And slander; the murder of Rizzio, Moray in that
And you behind Moray—the murder of Darnley,
    Throgmorton
Behind that too, you with them—and that winged
    scandal
You threw at us when we were married. Proof I have
    none
But I've felt it—would know it anywhere—in your
    eyes—
There—before me.

ELIZABETH: What may become a queen
Is to rule her kingdom. Had you ruled yours I'd say
She has her ways, I mine. Live and let live
And a merry world for those who have it. But now
I must think this over—sadness has touched your brain.
I'm no witch to charm you, make no incantations;
You came here by your own road.

MARY: I see how I came.
Back, back, each step the wrong way, and each sign
    followed
As you'd have me go, till the skein picks up and we
    stand

Face to face here. It was you forced Bothwell from
    me—
You there, and always. Oh, I'm to blame in this, too!
I should have seen your hand!

ELIZABETH: It has not been my use
To speak much or spend my time—

MARY: How could I have been
Mistaken in you for an instant?

ELIZABETH: You were not mistaken.
I am all women I must be. One's a young girl,
Young and harrowed as you are—one who could weep
To see you here—and one's a bitterness
At what I have lost and can never have, and one's
The basilisk you saw. This last stands guard
And I obey it. Lady, you came to Scotland
A fixed and subtle enemy, more dangerous
To me than you've ever known. This could not be
    borne,
And I set myself to cull you out and down,
And down you are.

MARY: When was I your enemy?

ELIZABETH: Your life was a threat to mine, your
    throne to my throne,
Your policy a threat.

MARY: How? Why?

ELIZABETH: It was you
Or I. Do you know that? The one of us must win

And I must always win. Suppose one lad
With a knife in his hand, a Romish lad who planted
That knife between my shoulders—my kingdom was
    yours.
It was too easy. You might not have wished it.
But you'd take it if it came.

MARY: And you'd take my life
And love to avoid this threat?

ELIZABETH: Nay, keep your life.
And your love, too. The lords have brought a parch-
    ment
For you to sign. Sign it and live.

MARY: If I sign it
Do I live where I please? Go free?

ELIZABETH: Nay, I would you might,
But you'd go to Bothwell, and between you two
You might be too much for Moray. You'll live with me
In London. There are other loves, my dear.
You'll find amusement there in the court. I assure you
It's better than a cell.

MARY: And if I will not sign
This abdication?

ELIZABETH: You've tasted prison. Try
A diet of it.

MARY: And so I will.

ELIZABETH: I can wait.

MARY: And I can wait. I can better wait than you.
Bothwell will fight free again. Kirkaldy
Will fight beside him, and others will spring up
From these dragon's teeth you've sown. Each week
   that passes
I'll be stronger, and Moray weaker.

ELIZABETH: And do you fancy
They'll rescue you from an English prison? Why,
Let them try it.

MARY: Even that they may do. I wait for
   Bothwell—
And wait for him here.

ELIZABETH: Where you will wait, bear in mind,
Is for me to say. Give up Bothwell, give up your
   throne
If you'd have a life worth living.

MARY: I will not.

ELIZABETH: I can wait.

MARY: And will not because you play to lose. This
   trespass
Against God's right will be known. The nations will
   know it,
Mine and yours. They will see you as I see you
And pull you down.

ELIZABETH: Child, child, I've studied this gambit
Before I play it. I will send each year

This paper to you. Not signing, you will step
From one cell to another, step lower always,
Till you reach the last, forgotten, forgotten of men,
Forgotten among causes, a wraith that cries
To fallen gods in another generation
That's lost your name. Wait then for Bothwell's rescue.
It will never come.

MARY: I may never see him?

ELIZABETH: Never.
It would not be wise.

MARY: And suppose indeed you won
Within our life-time, still looking down from the
    heavens
And up from men around us, God's spies that watch
The fall of great and little, they will find you out—
I will wait for that, wait longer than a life,
Till men and the times unscroll you, study the tricks
You play, and laugh, as I shall laugh, being known
Your better, haunted by your demon, driven
To death or exile by you, unjustly. Why,
When all's done, it's my name I care for, my name
    and heart,
To keep them clean. Win now, take your triumph
    now,
For I'll win men's hearts in the end—though the
    sifting takes
This hundred years—or a thousand.

ELIZABETH: Child, child, are you gulled
By what men write in histories, this or that,
And never true? I am careful of my name

As you are, for this day and longer. It's not what
    happens
That matters, no, not even what happens that's true,
But what men believe to have happened. They will
    believe
The worst of you, the best of me, and that
Will be true of you and me. I have seen to this.
What will be said about us in after-years
By men to come, I control that, being who I am.
It will be said of me that I governed well,
And wisely, but of you, cousin, that your life,
Shot through with ill-loves, battened on lechery, made
    you
An ensign of evil, that men tore down and trampled.
Shall I call for the lord's parchment?

    MARY: This will be said—?
But who will say it? It's a lie—will be known as a
    lie!

    ELIZABETH: You lived with Bothwell before Darnley
    died,
You and Bothwell murdered Darnley.

    MARY: And that's a lie!

    ELIZABETH: Your letters, my dear. Your letters to
    Bothwell prove it.
We have those letters.

    MARY: Then they're forged and false!
For I never wrote them!

    ELIZABETH: It may be they were forged.

But will that matter, Mary, if they're believed?
All history is forged.

MARY: You would do this?

ELIZABETH: It is already done.

MARY: And still I win.
A demon has no children, and you have none,
Will have none, can have none, perhaps. This crooked
    track
You've drawn me on, cover it, let it not be believed
That a woman was a fiend. Yes, cover it deep,
And heap my infamy over it, lest men peer
And catch sight of you as you were and are. In myself
I know you to be an eater of dust. Leave me here
And set me lower this year by year, as you promise,
Till the last is an oubliette, and my name inscribed
On the four winds. Still, STILL I win! I have been
A woman, and I have loved as a woman loves,
Lost as a woman loses. I have borne a son,
And he will rule Scotland—and England. You have no
    heir!
A devil has no children!

ELIZABETH: By God, you shall suffer
For this, but slowly.

MARY: And that I can do. A woman
Can do that. Come, turn the key. I have a hell
For you in mind, where you will burn and feel it,
Live where you live, and softly.

Dorothy 279
85
d Prejudice 237

, Terence 24, 285
, The 209
Rome, The 106
and Juliet 300

n, William 3
Duba 132
l Man, The 45
Service 90
th Seal, The 168
speare, William 176,

, George Bernard 97
dan, Richard Brinsley

wood, Robert 106
ing Prince, The 24
ates Wounded 266
is, Barrie 204

Time of Your Life, The 3
Trifles 262
Two Gentlemen of Verona,
The 176

Uncle Vanya 248
d'Usseau, Arnaud 279

Vanbrugh, Sir John 209
Van Druten, John 12
Venus Observed 117
Vortex, The 253

Waltz of the Toreadors, The
172
Way of the World, The 18
Werfel, Franz 138
Wilde, Oscar 111, 160
Williams, Tennessee 39
Woman of No Importance, A
160
Women, The 243

ELIZABETH: Once more I ask you,
And patiently. Give up your throne.

MARY: No, devil.
My pride is stronger than yours, and my heart beats
blood
Such as yours has never known. And in this dungeon,
I win here, alone.

ELIZABETH (*Turning*): Good night, then.

MARY: Aye, good night.
(ELIZABETH *goes to the door, which opens before her.*
She goes out slowly. As the door begins to close upon
her, MARY *calls.*) Beaton!

ELIZABETH (*Turning*): You will not see your maids
again,
I think. It's said they bring you news from the north.

MARY: I thank you for all kindness.
(ELIZABETH *goes out.* MARY *stands for a moment in*
thought, then walks to the wall and lays her hand
against the stone, pushing outward. The stone is cold,
and she shudders. Going to the window she sits again
in her old place and looks out into the darkness.
Curtain.)

Index

Anderson, Maxwell 306
Anouilh, Jean 172
Anthony, C. L. 291
Arms and the Man 97
Autumn Crocus 291
Autumn Garden, The 79

Bagnold, Enid 271
Barber of Seville, The 191
Beaumarchais 191
Behrman, S. N. 16, 45
Bergman, Ingmar 168
Boothe, Clare 243

Cage, The 127
Chalk Garden, The 271
Chekov, Anton 75, 248
Circle, The 67
Congreve, William 18
Coward, Nöel 253
Cymbeline 58

Daisy Miller 182
Death of a Salesman 221
Deputy, The 216
Doll's House, A 51
Duenna, The 197

Edward, My Son 145
Euripides 101

Fashion 34
Fratti, Mario 127
Friedman, Bruce Jay 132
Fry, Christopher 117

Gilbert, W
Gillette, W
Glaspell, S
Goat Song

Hellman, Li
Hochhuth, F

I Am a Came
Ibsen, Henrik

James, Henry
Jerome, Helen

Ladies of the C
279
Lady Winderme
Lamp at Midnig
Langley, Noel
Lavery, Emmet
Levinson, Alfred

Magnificent Yanke
122
Mary of Scotland
Master Builder, Th
Maugham, W. Som
Medea 101
Miller, Arthur 221
Moon for the Misbe
29
Morley, Robert 145
Mowatt, Anna Cora

O'Neill, Eugene 29
Orpheus Descending

318

Parker,
Patienc
Pride a

Rattiga
Relaps
Road t
Rome

Saroy
Scube
Secor
Secre
Seve
Shak
  3(
Sha
She
  1
She
Sle
Soc
Sta

DATE DUE

OCT 1 1 92			
OCT 2 4 1995			
MAR 16 1998			